Student's Book

Ben Goldstein & **Ceri Jones**
with **David McKeegan**

Starter Unit	Vocabulary		Language focus	
	p4 the alphabet, numbers, time, **p5** classroom objects, **p6** personal possessions and adjectives, **p7** days of the week, months and dates, **p8** countries, nationalities and languages		**p5** prepositions of place, *this, that, these, those*, **p6** possessive adjectives and possessive pronouns, possessive *'s*, **p7** *be*: affirmative, negative and questions	

Unit	Vocabulary	Reading	Language focus 1	Listening and vocabulary
1 People	**p11** Family and friends	**p12** An online article **Explore** adjectives	**p13** *have got* ▶ Robot fighters	**p14** A conversation Describing people
2 It's your life	**p21** Daily routines	**p22** An online forum **Explore** prepositions of time	**p23** present simple **Say it right!** /s/ /z/ /iz/ ▶ Ali's Day	**p24** After school activities A conversation **Get it right!** activities ending in *-ing*
	Review Unit 1 and 2 page 30–31			
3 Schooldays	**p33** Places in a school	**p34** A magazine article **Explore** nouns and verbs	**p35** *can* for ability and permission **Say it right!** *can/can't* ▶ Kung Fu school	**p36** A podcast School subjects
4 Food!	**p43** Food	**p44** A magazine article **Explore** expressions with *have 2*	**p45** countable and uncountable nouns, *a/an, some* and *any* ▶ Fishing in Japan	**p46** A conversation Meals and courses
	Review Unit 3 and 4 page 52–53			
5 Animal world	**p55** Animals **Get it right!** irregular plurals	**p56** A quiz **Explore** adverbs of movement	**p57** present continuous **Say it right!** /g/ and /ing/ sounds ▶ Shark attack	**p58** A conversation Action verbs
6 City life	**p65** Places in a town 1	**p66** An information text **Explore** extreme adjectives	**p67** *was / were, there was/were* **Get it right!** *any* ▶ Rome: ancient and modern	**p68** A report Places in a town 2
	Review Unit 5 and 6 page 74–75			
7 Sport	**p77** Sports and activities **Get it right!** *play* or *do*	**p78** FAQs **Explore** adverbs	**p79** past simple: *yes/no* questions **Say it right!** sentence stress ▶ The Palio	**p80** A conversation Clothes
8 Holidays	**p87** Seasons and weather	**p88** A web page **Explore** collocations	**p89** *be going to* **Say it right!** *going to* ▶ City of water	**p90** A conversation Landscapes
	Review Unit 7 and 8 page 96–97			

Projects p123–125   Irregular verbs and phonemic script p126

Speaking and listening				
p4 greetings,				
p9 ▶ Real Talk: What's your name? Where are you from? Asking for clarification				

Language focus 2	Discover Culture (Video and Reading)	Speaking	Writing	Extras
p15 Comparative adjectives Say it right! /ðən/	p16 ▶ My family, by Boris Moldanov p17 An online interview Explore adjective suffixes -ful	p18 ▶ Real Talk: What's your phone number? What's your email address? On the phone	p19 A description of a person Useful language: modifiers	p99 Grammar reference p107 Vocabulary bank p115 CLIL Maths – fractions ▶ The Land Down Under
p25 Present simple questions, Adverbs of frequency	p26 ▶ Chinese gymnast p27 A blog Explore expressions with have 1	p28 ▶ Real Talk: What do you do after school? Asking for information	p29 A blog post Useful language: modifiers	p100 Grammar reference p108 Vocabulary bank p116 CLIL Science – the Earth's movements ▶ Mars
p37 Object pronouns, (don't) like, don't mind, love, hate + ing	p38 ▶ South African schoolgirl p39 A profile Explore adjectives	p40 ▶ Real Talk: Can you use your mobile phone at school? Asking and giving permission	p41 An email Useful language: informal language	p101 Grammar reference p109 Vocabulary bank p117 CLIL Design and Technology – drawing tools ▶ Da Vinci's Design
p47 there is / there are, much / many / a lot of, how much/ many? Say it right! intonation in questions	p48 ▶ Dabbawallas p49 A magazine interview Explore International words	p50 ▶ Real Talk: What do you usually have for lunch? Ordering food	p51 A report Useful language: time connectors	p102 Grammar reference p110 Vocabulary bank p118 CLIL Geography – Climate and food ▶ Mountains of Rice
p59 Present simple vs present continuous Get it right! verbs that don't take present continuous	p60 ▶ Animals in the city p61 An article Explore the suffix -er	p62 ▶ Real Talk: Do you like going to museums? Asking for and giving directions	p63 A description of an animal Useful language: position of adjectives	p103 Grammar reference p111 Vocabulary bank p119 CLIL Science – vertebrates ▶ Chameleons
p69 Past simple: regular and irregular verbs Say it right! /t/, /d/ and /id/ ago	p70 ▶ Crossing cities p71 A blog Explore collocations	p72 ▶ Real Talk: Where do you usually go with your friends? Sequencing	p73 A description of a place Useful language: adding information	p104 Grammar reference p112 Vocabulary bank p120 CLIL Art – images and communication ▶ Big Art
p81 Past simple: Wh- questions Get it right! questions in the past tense	p82 ▶ The bowler p83 An article Explore irregular plurals	p84 ▶ Real Talk: What's your favourite sport and why? Expressing interest Get it right! American and British English words	p85 A biography Useful language: prepositions of time and place	p105 Grammar reference p113 Vocabulary bank p121 CLIL PE – outdoor sports and activities ▶ Extreme Fishing
p91 Future with will/ won't	p92 ▶ Alaska p93 An information brochure Explore adjectives	p94 ▶ Real Talk: Where do you like going on holiday? Making suggestions	p95 An email Useful language: starting and finishing an email	p106 Grammar reference p114 Vocabulary bank p122 CLIL Maths – frequency tables and bar charts ▶ Holiday in Australia

Starter Unit

Greetings

1 Complete the conversation with the phrases below.

> What's your name?   Hi!
> Nice to meet you,   I'm

Jane: ¹....
Mark: Hello.
Jane: ²....
Mark: I'm Mark. What's your name?
Jane: ³.... Jane.
Mark: ⁴...., Jane.
Jane: Nice to meet you, too!

2 🔊 1.01 Listen, check, and repeat the conversation in pairs.

The alphabet

3 🔊 1.02 Listen and repeat.

A B C D E F G
H I J K L M N
O P Q R S T U
V W X Y Z

4 💬 Work in small groups. Ask and answer the question and write the answers.

> How do you spell your name?

> M-A-R-I-A

Numbers

5 Write the calculations as words.

a *one + eight = nine*

a) 1 + 8 =   d) 7 − 3 =
b) 4 + 6 =   e) 9 × 2 =
c) 8 − 5 =   f) 10 ÷ 5 =

6 🔊 1.03 Listen and check.

7 Put the numbers in order from low to high.

8 🔊 1.04 Listen and check.

9 💬 Work with a partner. Ask and answer *How old are you?*

> How old are you?

> I'm ..... How old are you?

Time

10 Match the times with the clocks.

1 Midnight
2 A quarter past five
3 Ten to three
4 Half past ten
5 Five o'clock
6 A quarter to seven
7 Half past two

Your turn

11 Ask and answer with your partner.
1 What time is it now?
2 What time is your English lesson?
3 What time is your first lesson in the morning?
4 What time is your last lesson in the afternoon?

Prepositions

1 Match the prepositions and phrases with the pictures.

> behind   in   in front of
> ~~between~~   next to   on

1 *between*

Classroom objects

2 Find the words in the box in the picture.

> bag   board   books   bookshelf   desk
> dictionary   laptop   notebook   pen
> pencil   pencil sharpener   rubber   ruler

3 Write questions and answers about the picture in Exercise 2.

1 *Where's the notebook?*
   It's on the desk.

1 notebook   5 books
2 white rubber   6 laptop
3 red pencil   7 bag
4 board

Your turn

4 Work with a partner. Look round your classroom. Ask and answer questions about where classroom objects are.

> Where's the board?
>
> It's behind the teacher.

this, *that*, *these* and *those*

5 Look at the pictures. Complete the sentences with *this*, *that*, *these* or *those*.

That is my mum.

…. are my books.

…. are my blue shoes.

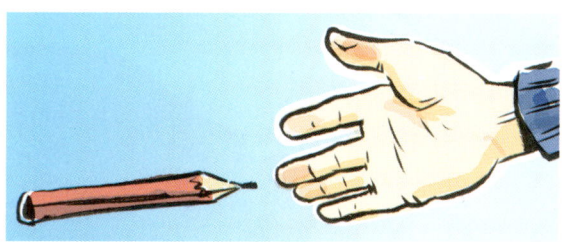

…. is my pencil.

Possessive adjectives and possessive pronouns

subject pronouns	possessive adjectives	possessive pronouns
I	my	mine
….	your	yours
he	his	his
….	her	hers
it	its	–
we	our	….
you	….	yours
….	their	theirs

➡ **Grammar reference** • page 98

1 Complete the table with the correct words.

2 Circle the correct words.
1 He / **It** is I / **my** ruler. He's / **It's** blue.
2 It's **her** / she laptop. She's / It's new.
3 That's not you / your phone. It's my / mine.
4 They / Their are we / our books.
5 It isn't him / his brother. It's her / hers.
6 That is they / their dictionary.
7 You're / Your my friend.

Personal possessions and adjectives

3 Match the pictures with the words in the box.

> a nice car   a new skateboard   a small bike
> a big bike   ~~an expensive computer~~
> an old mobile phone

1 *an expensive computer*

Possessive 's

> Use a name or a noun + 's to show possession.
> *My brother's laptop.*

➡ **Grammar reference** • page 98

4 Write sentences with the possessive 's.
1 *My sister's bike is new.*

1 My / sister / bike / is / new.

2 Jake / computer / is / great!

3 My / mum / car / is / small.

4 My / brother / skateboard / is / old.

5 Kate / new / book / is / big.

be: affirmative, negative and questions

	+	−	
I	am	'm not	
He/She/It	….	isn't	12.
We/You/They	are	aren't	

?			+	−
….	I		Yes, I am.	No, I'm not.
Is	he/she/it	12?	Yes, he/she/it is.	No, he/she/it isn't.
….	we/you/they		Yes, we/you/they are.	No, we/you/they aren't.

➡ **Grammar reference • page 98**

1 Complete the table with the correct forms of the verb *be*.

2 Complete the sentences with the correct form of the verb *be*.

1 *'m*

1 I …. Paul.
2 She …. Sara.
3 We …. friends.
4 You …. Tim.
5 They …. Pete and Suzie.
6 He …. a teacher.
7 You …. the students in my class.
8 It …. a dictionary.

3 Make the sentences in Exercise 2 negative.

1 *I'm not Paul.*

4 Write questions with *be*.

1 *Are you David?*

1 you / David?
2 we / in English class?
3 it / cold today?
4 the school / big?
5 you / eleven?
6 the teachers / children?

Your turn

5 Work with a partner. Ask and answer the questions in Exercise 4.

Are you David?   *No, I'm not. I'm John.*

Days of the week

6 Put the days of the week in the correct order.

Friday   Saturday   Monday   Sunday   Tuesday   Wednesday   Thursday

7 🔊 1.05 Listen and check.

Months and dates

8 Complete the months with the missing letters.

J _ n _ _ ry   J _ ly
F _ bru _ ry   A _ g _ st
M _ rch   S _ pt _ mb _ r
Apr _ l   Oct _ b _ r
M _ y   N _ v _ mb _ r
J _ ne   D _ c _ mb _ r

9 🔊 1.06 Listen and repeat.

10 Match the dates.

1 *c*

1 24/7   A January 24
2 1/5   B September 1
3 1/9   C July 24
4 24/1   D March 8
5 17/8   E May 1
6 17/12   F February 12
7 8/3   G December 17
8 12/2   H August 17

11 🔊 1.07 Listen and check.

Your turn

12 Ask and answer with your partner.

1 What month is it?
2 When's your birthday?
3 What's your favourite month?
4 When are your parents' birthdays?

Countries, nationalities and languages

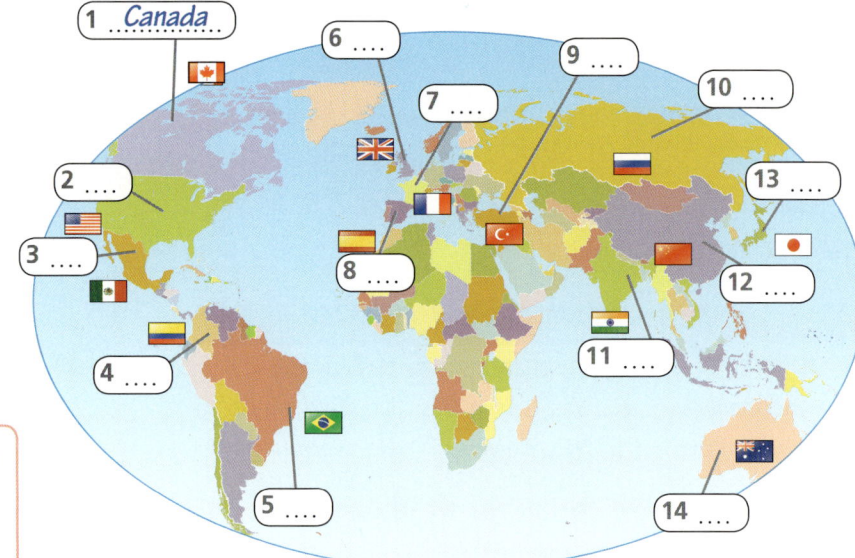

1 Canada
2 ....
3 ....
4 ....
5 ....
6 ....
7 ....
8 ....
9 ....
10 ....
11 ....
12 ....
13 ....
14 ....

1 Label the countries on the map.

> Australia   Brazil   Britain   ~~Canada~~
> China   Colombia   France   India
> Japan   Mexico   Russia   Spain
> Turkey   the USA

2 🔊 **1.08** Listen, check and repeat.

3 Complete the table with the correct nationalities.

Country	Nationality	Country	Nationality
America	American	Russia	4 ....
Australia	Australian	Britain	British
Brazil	1	Turkey	Turkish
Canada	Canadian	Spain	5 ....
Colombia	2	China	Chinese
India	3	Japan	6 ....
Mexico	Mexican	France	French

4 🔊 **1.09** Listen, check and repeat.

5 Write sentences about the people below.

1 *Yuki's from Japan. She's Japanese.*
2 *Michel and Nicole are from France. They're French.*

1 Yuki … Japan
2 Michel and Nicole … France
3 Sarah … Australia
4 Li Ping … China
5 Vlad and Oksana … Russia
6 Raj and Sanjeet … India
7 Harry … America
8 Leticia and Pedro … Mexico

6 💬 Where are you from? Ask and answer with your partner.

7 Do the quiz.

1 What nationality is Harry Styles?

2 What country is this from?
3 What are the two official languages of Canada?

4 Where is this city?

5 What language is this?
6 Where is Beijing?

8 Compare your answers with your partner.

Speaking Asking for clarification

Real Talk: What's your name? Where are you from?

Name	Nationality	Parents' nationality
Rachel	British	British
Binnie	British	British
Steven	….	Mum: …. Dad: Israeli
Emily	….	Mum: American Dad: ….
Courtney	….	Mum: …. Dad: ….
Freddie	….	Mum: …. Dad: English

1 ▶ 0.1 Watch the teenagers in the video. Complete the chart on the right.

2 💬 What's *your* name? Where are *you* from?

3 🔊 1.10 Listen to the conversation. When is Janek's birthday?

Useful language

So, your name is (Janek), is that right?
Yes, that's right.
How do you spell that?

Sorry,
Can you repeat that please?
Of course.

4 Look at the Useful language box and complete the conversation.

> repeat ~~right~~ course Sorry spell

1 *right*

Teacher:	So, your first name is **Janek** and your surname is **Czerwinski**, is that ¹…. ?
Janek:	Yes, that's right.
Teacher:	How do you ²…. that?
Janek:	It's **C Z E R W I N S K I**.
Teacher:	OK, thanks. And where are you from?
Janek:	**Katowice**, in **Poland**. That's **K A T O W I C E**.
Teacher:	And what's your date of birth?
Janek:	**12th April 2000**.
Teacher:	³…. , can you ⁴…. that please?
Janek:	Yes, of ⁵…. . It's **12th April 2000**.
Teacher:	Thanks. And what's your address here in Bristol?
Janek:	**24 Walton Street**.

5 🔊 1.10 Listen, check and practise the conversation with your partner.

6 💬 Change the words in bold in the conversation in Exercise 4. Use the information on the cards. Practise the conversation.

Student ID Card
BRUNO NEUMANN
from: Munich, Germany
dob: 23rd May 1999
address in Bristol: 10 Clifton Street

Student ID Card
DANDAN LOENG
from: Hangzhou, China
dob: 16th August 2000
address in Bristol: 21 Kings Gardens

1 People

In this unit ...

Robot fighters **p13**

My family **p16**

On the phone **p18**

CLIL The land down under **p115**

Vocabulary
- Family and friends
- Describing people
- Adjectives

Language focus
- *have got* affirmative, negative, questions and short answers
- Comparative adjectives

Unit aims
I can ...
- talk about my family.
- compare people.
- understand a text about other cultures.
- talk on the phone.
- write a description of someone.
- write an email about my school.

BE CURIOUS

What can you see in the photo?
Start thinking
- How many people are in this family?
- How old do you think they are?
- When do you wear boots like these?

Vocabulary Family and friends

1 Look at the family tree. Where is Sarah?

2 🔊 1.11 Complete the text with the words in the box. Then listen, check and repeat.

> uncle   brother   aunt   teammates   wife   dad   cousin   sister   classmates
> grandma   granddad   mum   best friend   parents   ~~grandparents~~

Here's a picture of my family and friends. At the top are my ¹ *grandparents* .
My ² …'s name is David and his ³ … is Betty. She's my ⁴ … . My ⁵ …'s name is Helen and my ⁶ … is Richard. They are my ⁷ … . Paul is my ⁸ … and Kate is my ⁹ … . Jessie is my ¹⁰ … . Our ¹¹ …'s name is Tony. I've got one ¹² … – his name is Charlie. At the bottom of the picture is my ¹³ … , Jade, my ¹⁴ … (we play netball for our school), and my ¹⁵ … – I just call them 'the guys'!

3 Look at the family tree again and complete the sentences with the words in the box.

> son   daughter   grandson   granddaughter

1 *Sarah is David and Betty's daughter.*

1 Sarah is David and Betty's … .
2 Charlie is Jessie and Tony's … .
3 Kate is Richard and Helen's … .
4 Paul is David and Betty's … .

4 Copy and complete the circles with the words in Exercise 2.

Your turn

5 Draw your family tree. Tell your partner who the people are.

> These are my grandparents. Their names are Manuel and Carla. That's my dad …

 Vocabulary bank • page 107

A VERY BIG FAMILY!

Have you got a brother or a sister? How many have you got? One? Two? Maybe more?

Damien Baxter is very lucky. He's got fourteen brothers and sisters!

The family lives in a big house in Western Australia. The house has got seven bedrooms, and lots of beds. It isn't a quiet house. It's a very noisy house with lots of children in it.

Three of Damien's brothers and sisters are adults. They've got children too. Damien is a baby, but he's an uncle to those children!

The Baxter family is very busy. There's lots of work to do in the Baxter house. When a child is eight years old, they help with the work. Damien is only three months old, so he hasn't got jobs to do yet.

They haven't got a car. Damien's dad's got a bus! It's got sixteen seats.

The Baxters are a very happy family, and the kids are all good friends.

FACT! The average number of children in Australian families is 1.9.

Reading An online article

1 Look at the photo and the title of this article. What is special about this family?

2 🔊 1.12 Read the article. Is it a happy family?

3 Read the text again. Are the sentences true (*T*) or false (*F*)? Correct the false ones.
   1 Damien is not a baby. *F – Damien is a baby.*
   2 There are fifteen boys in the family.
   3 Three of his brothers and sisters aren't children.
   4 Damien's house is very quiet.
   5 The children aren't very good friends.

Explore adjectives

4 Find the opposites of these adjectives in the text.
   1 unlucky *lucky*   3 quiet   5 bad
   2 small   4 unhappy

Your turn

5 Write notes about your family and Damien's family.

My family	Damien's family
small	big

6 Tell your partner about how your family is different from Damien's family.

Language focus 1 *have got*

1 Complete the examples from the text on page 12.

	I / We / You / They	He / She / It
+	They .... fifteen children.	The house **has got** seven bedrooms.
–	They haven't got a car.	Damien .... jobs to do.
?	Have you got a brother or a sister?	**Has** he **got** a house?
+	Yes, I have.	Yes, he **has**.
–	No, I haven't.	No, he .... .

➔ Grammar reference • page 99

2 Complete the text about Nicole's family. Use the correct form of *have got*.

This is me and my family. I ¹.... two brothers. I ².... (not) a sister. Those are my parents. We ³.... a big garden. My dad ⁴.... one brother, my Uncle Matt. My uncle ⁵.... three boys. That's their dog, Lady. It loves our big garden. We ⁶.... (not) a dog. And my cousins ⁷.... (not) a big garden.

3 Look at the pictures of James and Alice. Write questions and answers.
  1 *Has James got a book about sport?*
    Yes, he has.
 1 James / a book about sport?
 2 Alice / a computer?
 3 James / black trainers?
 4 Alice / a skateboard?
 5 James / blue headphones?
 6 Alice / a CD?
 7 James / a hat ?

4 💬 Work with a partner. Ask and answer the questions from Exercise 3.

Your turn

5 Work with a partner. Ask and answer questions about what you have got. Complete the chart and add your own ideas.

	You	Your partner
a brother		
a sister		
a cat		
a computer		
a skateboard		
....		
....		

Have you got a brother?   Yes, I have.

Learn about another unusual family in Japan.
 • How many robots has the Suni family got?
 • What colour is Arina's robot?

1.1 Robot fighters

Listening A conversation

1 Look at the picture. What things have the avatars got?

2 🔊 1.13 Listen to the conversation between Connor and Suzi. Which is Connor's avatar?

3 🔊 1.13 Listen again. Correct the sentences.
  1 The game is called 'My 3D house'.
  2 Connor is on level 15.
  3 Connor has got ten stars.
  4 Suzi's avatar has got a blue skateboard.

Vocabulary Describing people

4 🔊 1.14 Choose the correct words from the box. Then listen, check and repeat.

> funny   brown   intelligent   short
> blue   straight   good-looking   old

1 *straight*

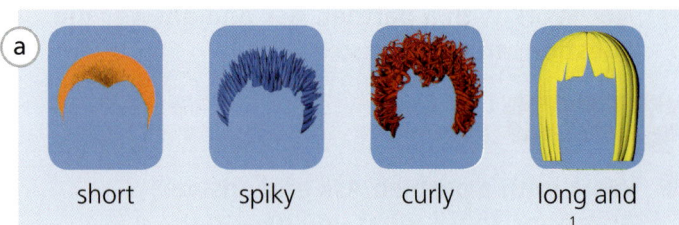

a short | spiky | curly | long and ¹....

b fair | dark | ² ....

c green | brown | ³ ....

d tall | ⁴ ....

e pretty | ⁵ ....

f ⁶ .... | young

Your turn

5 Invent an avatar. Write a description. Read it to the class.
  My avatar is tall. She's got spiky hair. It's green. She's got brown eyes.
  ➔ **Vocabulary bank** • page 107

g ⁷ .... | ⁸ ....

14

Language focus 2
Comparative adjectives

1 Complete the examples from the listening on page 14.

Comparative
long longer
It's .... your hair.
tall taller
You're .... me.

➡ Grammar reference • page 99

👁 Get it right!
One-syllable adjectives ending in a single consonant: double the consonant.
big – bigger   red – redder

2 Complete the table with the correct form of the adjective.

Adjective	Comparative
1 short	....
2	curlier
3 dark	....
4	better
5 beautiful	....
6 young	....
7	older
8	more intelligent
9 pretty	....

3 Complete the sentences. Use the comparative form of the adjective in brackets.
1 My hair is .... (curly) your hair.
2 My dad is .... (old) my mum.
3 You are .... (intelligent) your brother.
4 His story is .... (funny) my story.
5 Are you .... (tall) me?
6 Her hair is .... (straight) your hair.

Say it right!
/ðən/

🔊 **1.15** Listen and repeat the sentences.
1 My hair is shorter than your hair.
2 My mum is older than my dad.
3 Are you taller than me?
4 Fred is more intelligent than Josh.

4 Look at the picture. Write sentences with the comparative form of the adjectives below.

big   small   straight   pretty   long   noisy   quiet

Patch   Libby

1 *Patch is bigger than Libby.*

Your turn

5 Work with a partner. Write sentences comparing yourself to him/her. Use these adjectives and other adjectives you can think of.

young   old   funny   tall   short   intelligent

I'm younger than Silvia.

Discover Culture

1 Look at the map and the pictures. Where's Siberia? Find **six** of these things in the photos. Check the meanings of the other words.

> bear boat dancing fire forest Khanti people
> reindeer singing sleigh snow snowmobile sunshine

2 Which of the things in Exercise 1 do you think are in the video?

3 **1.2** Watch the video without sound and check your answers to Exercise 1.

Find out about a Siberian boy.

1.2 My family, by Boris Moldanov

4 **1.2** Watch the video up to 0.58 with sound. Choose the best summary for the first part of the video.
- A small town in Siberia
- Siberian weather and wildlife
- Fun in Siberia

5 **1.2** Watch the video from 1.18 to the end. Put the events in order.
a) They ride on a sleigh with reindeer.
b) They travel on a snowmobile.
c) They dance around a fire.

6 **1.2** Watch the video again. Are the sentences true (*T*) or false (*F*)?
1 Boris' grandparents' house is smaller than Boris' house.
2 They've got about 500 reindeer.
3 The town has one shop and two roads.
4 Boris' father and sister visit his grandparents.
5 The trip takes three hours.
6 It's hard work and fun at his grandparents' house.
7 The film finishes with a sleigh ride.

Your turn

7 Compare Boris' town, shops and family with yours. Complete the table.

	Weather	Towns	Shops	Family
Me				*two sisters*
Boris	cold	small	1	one brother

8 Work with a partner. Talk about your answers to Exercise 7.

> My family is bigger than Boris'. I've got two sisters.

> Our town is bigger than Boris' town.

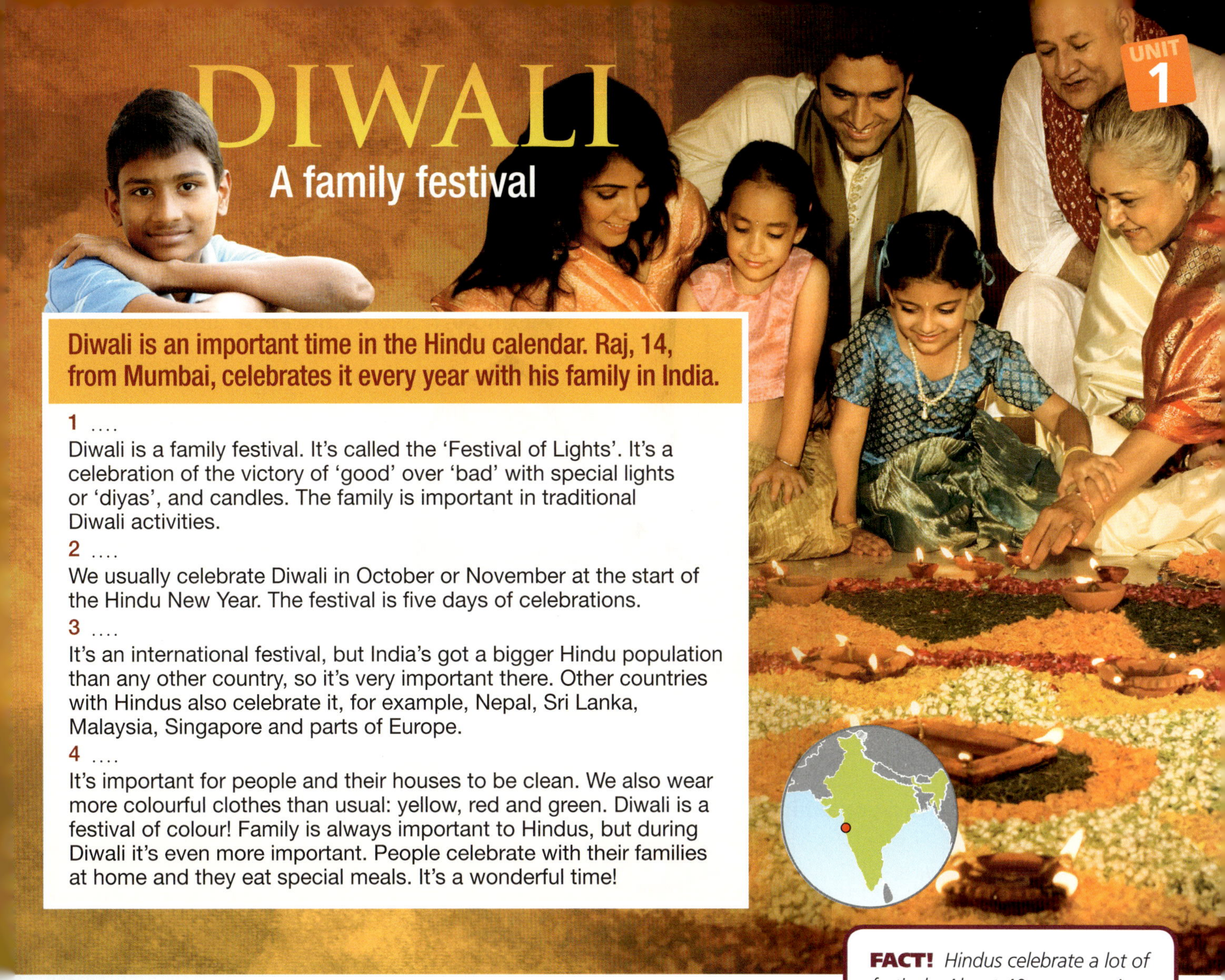

DIWALI
A family festival

Diwali is an important time in the Hindu calendar. Raj, 14, from Mumbai, celebrates it every year with his family in India.

1 ....
Diwali is a family festival. It's called the 'Festival of Lights'. It's a celebration of the victory of 'good' over 'bad' with special lights or 'diyas', and candles. The family is important in traditional Diwali activities.

2 ....
We usually celebrate Diwali in October or November at the start of the Hindu New Year. The festival is five days of celebrations.

3 ....
It's an international festival, but India's got a bigger Hindu population than any other country, so it's very important there. Other countries with Hindus also celebrate it, for example, Nepal, Sri Lanka, Malaysia, Singapore and parts of Europe.

4 ....
It's important for people and their houses to be clean. We also wear more colourful clothes than usual: yellow, red and green. Diwali is a festival of colour! Family is always important to Hindus, but during Diwali it's even more important. People celebrate with their families at home and they eat special meals. It's a wonderful time!

FACT! Hindus celebrate a lot of festivals. About 40 every year!

Reading   An online interview

1 Look at the picture. Where is Raj from?

2 Read the interview. What is Diwali?

3 🔊 1.16 Complete the text with the questions.
- a) Where is it?
- b) When is it?
- c) What's important in Diwali?
- d) What is Diwali?

4 Read the text again. Choose the correct answers.
1. Diwali is a celebration of **the family / good**.
2. 'Diyas' are special **lights / candles**.
3. People celebrate for **two months / five days** during Diwali.
4. **People all over the world / Only Indian people** celebrate Diwali.
5. Colourful **clothes / houses** are very important at Diwali time.

Explore adjective suffixes -ful

5 Find two adjectives in the text which end in -ful.

➡ Vocabulary bank • page 107

6 Complete the sentences with the adjectives from Exercise 5.
1. This is a .... book – I love it!
2. My room is all white. I want it to be more ..... .

7 Change the nouns into adjectives by adding -ful.
beauty ....   use ....

Your turn

8 Write notes about a festival in your country. Use these headings:
- Activities
- Food
- Clothes
- Time of year

9 Tell your partner about your festival.

> The Barranquilla Carnival is a folk festival in my country. ...

Speaking On the phone

Real Talk: What's your phone number? What's your email address?

1 **1.3** Watch the teenagers in the video. Write their phone numbers and email addresses.

	Phone number	Email address
1 Petra	....	petraiscool@....
2 Stephen	....	....@schoolemail.com
3 Rachel	....	racheljane@....
4 Freddie	....	bertie13@....

2 What's *your* phone number? What's *your* email address? Ask and answer with your partner.

3 **1.17** Listen to the conversation. What does Raj want to do?

4 Complete the conversation with the useful language.

Useful language

Just a minute.   Hello?
Can I call you back?   Hi, it's Raj.

5 **1.17** Listen again and check your answers.

6 Work with a partner. Practise the conversation in Exercise 4.

7 Change the words in bold in the conversation in Exercise 4. Use the information below. Practise the conversation.

Lydia:	¹.... ?
Raj:	².... . How are you?
Lydia:	Hi Raj. OK, thanks. And you?
Raj:	Fine, thanks. Listen, have you got **Pablo's** phone number?
Lydia:	Um, yes. ³.... . It's **0273 270 895**.
Raj:	Thanks. I want to invite him to my Diwali party. Have you got his email, too?
Lydia:	I think so. Oh wait. Someone's at the door. ⁴.... ?
Raj:	Sure. Talk to you later. Bye.
Lydia:	Bye.

Maria: 0899 307 491
Email: mdulce10@netmail.net

Ramon: 0711 456 789
Email: imramon5@anon.net

Alex: 0565 171 806
Email: alex01@telefonika.com

Victoria: 0217 222 517
Email: vbrava@mymail.net

Writing A description of a person

1 Look at the photo and read the text. Who is writing the description?

MY BEST FRIEND

THIS WEEK: Javier Ramos from Cuenca, Spain.

My best friend is my brother, David. He's 20. He lives with me, my mum and my dad. David is taller than me. He's got dark hair and green eyes. He's very intelligent, and quite funny, too!

My brother's great, and he's a very good friend.

2 Copy and complete the table for Javier.

	Javier's best friend	Your best friend
Name	David	
Age		
Home	with Mum and Dad	
Description		

Useful language

Modifiers

not very   quite   really/very

3 Find examples of modifiers in Javier's description.

4 Complete the sentences with modifiers so they are true for you.
1 I'm .... tall.
2 My dad is .... intelligent.
3 My best friend is .... good-looking.
4 My English teacher is .... funny.

Get Writing

PLAN

5 Make notes about your best friend in the table in Exercise 2.

WRITE

6 Write a description of your best friend. Use your notes and the language below.
My best friend is …
He/She's not very / quite / really / very …
He/She's got …
He's/She's taller/shorter than …

CHECK

7 Can you say YES to these questions?
- Have you got information from Exercise 5 in your description?
- Have you got modifiers?
- Are your spelling, grammar and vocabulary correct?

2 It's your life

Discovery EDUCATION

In this unit …

Ali's day **p23**

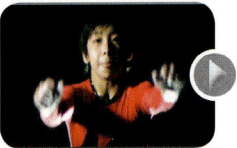
Zhin Yan: gymnast **p26**

After school activities **p28**

CLIL Mars **p116**

Vocabulary
- Daily routines and time expressions
- After school activities
- Prepositions of time
- Expressions with *have* 1

Language focus
- Present simple: affirmative and negative
- Adverbs of frequency
- Present simple: *Yes/No* and *Wh-* questions

Unit aims
I can …
- talk about daily routines.
- read and understand a text about time zones.
- have a conversation about after school activities.
- ask questions about routines and activities.
- understand about schools in other countries.
- ask for and give information about timetables.
- write a blog post about my typical day.
- use basic conjunctions.

BE CURIOUS

What can you see in the photo?
Start thinking
- Where are the children?
- Why are the girls clapping?
- Can you play a musical instrument?

Vocabulary Daily routines

1 🔊 **1.18** Match the pictures with the phrases. Then listen, check and repeat.

- *a* do some exercise
- .... have lunch
- .... get dressed
- .... get up
- .... go to bed
- .... brush my teeth
- .... have a shower
- .... go to school
- .... have breakfast
- .... do my homework

2 Complete the text with phrases from Exercise 1.

A day in my life

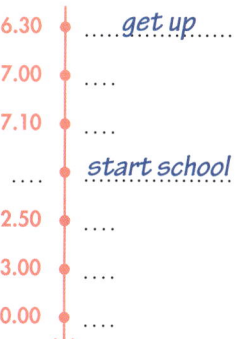

Hi, I'm Cecilia and I'm from Chile. I ¹ *get up* at 6.30 in the morning on schooldays. I ² .... a shower and then I ³ .... dressed. At 7.00, I ⁴ .... breakfast. After breakfast I ⁵ .... my teeth, then I go to school with my brother at 7.15. We start school at 7.45. At 2.50 we go home and we ⁶ .... lunch with Mum. Then I ⁷ .... my homework in my bedroom, usually at about 3.00. I ⁸ .... some exercise or sport every day – basketball is my favourite sport. I ⁹ .... to bed at 10.00 on school nights, and 11.00 at the weekend.

3 🔊 **1.19** Listen and check.

4 Complete Cecilia's timeline.

- 6.30 *get up*
- 7.00 ....
- 7.10 ....
- ....   start school
- 2.50 ....
- 3.00 ....
- 10.00 ....

Your turn

5 Make your own timeline. Use the phrases from Exercise 1.

get up   7.30
have a shower   7.35

6 Work with a partner. Report your partner's answers to the class.

> Shilan gets up at 7.30.

> Mika has breakfast at …

➡ **Vocabulary bank • page 108**

Times around the world

FACT! The first country in the world to see a new day is the Republic of Kiribati – an island in the Pacific Ocean.

the UK

Marta Hello! I'm at school with my friend, May. We're in the dining hall. We walk to school together in the morning and at lunchtime we always eat together. Sometimes we study together.

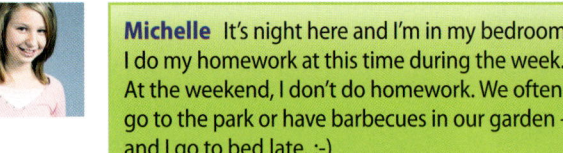

Michelle It's night here and I'm in my bedroom. I do my homework at this time during the week. At the weekend, I don't do homework. We often go to the park or have barbecues in our garden – and I go to bed late. :-)
....

Renata Wow, is it really night there, Michelle? Amazing! I start school at this time. I'm in the school library now. I don't like school. :-(My dad teaches at my school, so we go there together.
....

David Hi Renata! Hi Marta! Hi Michelle! I'm at home. I usually eat with my mum and my brother at this time. My brother is two years old. He doesn't go to school. I love playing with my brother – he's funny! We sleep in the afternoon and we go out at night because it's very hot here.
....

Reading An online forum

1 Look at the time zone map. When it's 12 (noon) in London, what time is it in Sydney?

2 🔊 **1.20** Read the online forum. Match the people to the cities on the map.

3 Read the text again. Complete the sentences with Marta, Renata, David or Michelle.
1 _Renata_ and .... are at school.
2 .... and .... are at home.
3 .... does homework at this time.
4 .... has lunch at this time.
5 .... doesn't like school.
6 .... goes to school with a friend.

Explore prepositions of time

4 Find examples of prepositions of time in the reading text.
at lunchtime

5 Write the correct preposition, then complete the sentences for you.
1 _In the morning, I do some exercise._

1 .... the morning, ...
2 .... lunchtime, ...
3 .... the weekend, ...
4 .... the afternoon, ...
5 .... night, ...

➔ **Vocabulary bank** • page 108

Your turn

6 Look at the times in the cities below. What time is it in your country? Tell your partner where you are at that time.
1 It's 12 noon in London.
   It's midnight here. I'm in bed.
2 It's 3 am in Rio.
3 It's 6 pm in Dubai.
4 It's 2 pm in Sydney.

Language focus 1 Present simple

1 Complete the examples from the text on page 22.

	I / We / You / They	He / She / It
+	I **start** school at this time. We .... to school together.	David **goes** to school.
–	We **don't walk** to school together.	He .... go to school.

➡ Grammar reference • page 100

2 Look at the examples, then write the *he/she/it* forms of the verbs.

walk – walk**s**
go – go**es**
teach – teach**es**
stud**y** – stud**ies**

1 brush ....
2 start ....
3 love ....
4 sleep ....
5 watch ....
6 do ....

Say it right!

🔊 1.21 Listen and complete the table with the words from Exercise 2.

/s/	/z/	/iz/
walk**s**	go**es**	teach**es**
....	....	....
....	....	....

🔊 1.21 Listen, check and repeat.

3 🔊 1.22 Complete Murat's blog entry with the correct form of the present simple. Then listen and check.

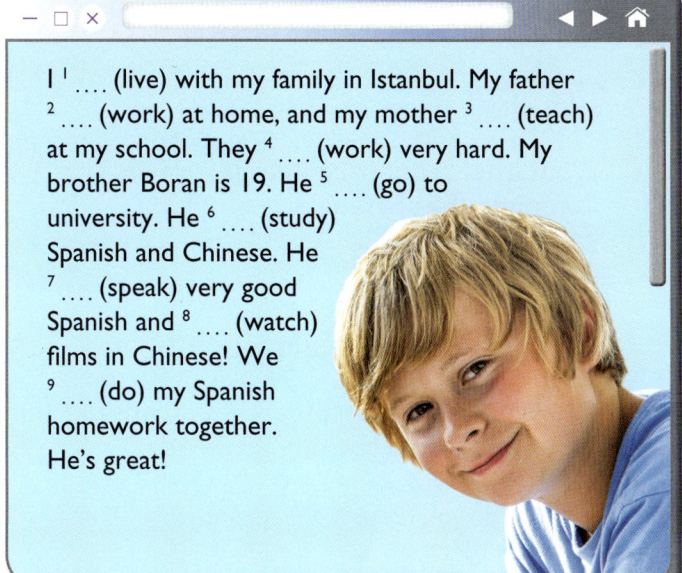

I ¹.... (live) with my family in Istanbul. My father ².... (work) at home, and my mother ³.... (teach) at my school. They ⁴.... (work) very hard. My brother Boran is 19. He ⁵.... (go) to university. He ⁶.... (study) Spanish and Chinese. He ⁷.... (speak) very good Spanish and ⁸.... (watch) films in Chinese! We ⁹.... (do) my Spanish homework together. He's great!

1 *live*

4 Read the texts on page 22 again. Correct the sentences below. One of them is correct.

1 *Renata's dad doesn't work at home. He works at her school.*

1 Renata's dad works at home.
2 Marta walks to school with her friend.
3 David has lunch at school.
4 Michelle does homework at the weekend.
5 David's brother goes to school.
6 Renata likes school.

Your turn

5 Make a list of things you do and don't do during the week, at weekends and every day.

During the week, I …	At weekends, I …	I … every day.
+	+	+
do my homework.		
–	–	–
	don't go to school	

6 Tell your partner about the things you do and don't do.

> During the week, I do my homework.

Find out about Ali's daily routine in Cairo.
• When does Ali wake up?
• What does Ali do during the day?
• What does he do in the evenings?

2.1 Ali's day

Vocabulary After school activities

1 🔊 1.23 Match the words to the pictures. Then listen, check and repeat.

_5_ play football
.... play music
.... do karate
.... play tennis
.... go swimming
.... do drama
.... have dance classes
.... have art classes
.... play chess

Listening A conversation

2 🔊 1.24 Listen to Clara and Lucas talking to their teacher. What activities do Clara and Lucas do?

3 🔊 1.24 Listen again. Choose the correct answers.

1 Lucas plays …
   a tennis   **b** chess
2 He plays with …
   a his teacher   b his friends
3 Clara has tennis lessons …
   a at school   b at the tennis club
4 She has lessons on …
   a Mondays and Thursdays
   b Mondays and Wednesdays
5 Clara's dad …
   a is good at tennis   b isn't good at tennis

> **Get it right!**
> Use *go* for activities ending in *-ing*.
> *go swimming, go running*

Your turn

4 What after school activities do you do? Complete the sentences.

On Fridays, I .... .
I .... at the weekend.
On ...., in the evening, I .... .
I .... in the morning on .... .

5 💬 Work with a partner. Ask and answer the questions in Exercise 4.

— What do you do at the weekend?
— At the weekend, I have dance classes.

Vocabulary bank • page 108

Language focus 2 Present simple questions

1 Complete the examples from the listening on page 24.

	I / We / You / They	He / She / It
Yes/No	…. you **do** any sports? …., I **do**. / No, I **don't**. **Do** Carla and her dad **play** tennis? Yes, they …. / …., they **don't**.	**Does** your dad …. tennis? Yes, he …. . / No, he **doesn't**.
Wh-	Where …. you play? What **do** they **play**?	Where **does** Lucas **play** chess? He **plays** at school and at home.

→ Grammar reference • page 100

2 💬 Choose the correct form of *do*. Ask and answer the questions with your partner.
1 Do / Does you play tennis?
2 Do / Does your friends have dance classes?
3 Do / Does your friend play football?
4 Do / Does you do karate?
5 Do / Does your sister play music?

Your turn

3 Copy and complete the table. Write a tick (✓) or a cross (✗). Ask your partner and complete the table for him or her.

Activities	You	Your partner
play tennis		
play chess		
do karate		
have dance classes		
play music		

> Do you play tennis?

> No, I don't.

Wh- questions

4 Look at the grammar table in Exercise 1 and complete the questions.
1 Who …. you live with?
2 Where …. your family live?
3 What time …. you get up in the morning?
4 What …. you and your friends do after school?
5 When …. you do sport?

5 💬 Work with a partner. Ask and answer the questions in Exercise 4.

Adverbs of frequency

always   usually   often   sometimes   never
I **often** play tennis with my dad.
I **sometimes** play tennis at school.
I'm **never** late for school.

Adverbs of frequency come after the verb **be** but before other verbs.
We ask questions about frequency with *How often …?*
How often do you play chess?

Your turn

6 Add adverbs of frequency to the sentences below to make them true for you.
1 I brush my teeth after breakfast.
   I always brush my teeth after breakfast.
2 I get up early at the weekend.
3 I play sports after school.
4 I watch TV in bed.
5 I am late for school.
6 I do my homework in the morning.

7 Ask and answer *How often* questions with your partner. Use the information in Exercise 6.

> How often do you watch TV in bed?

> I never watch TV in bed.

Discover Culture

1 **Look at the pictures of the schoolgirl, Zhin Yan, and answer the questions.**
   1 Where is she from?
   2 What sport do you think it is?
   3 Do you think the sport is easy or difficult?

Find out about a specialist school in Beijing.

2.2 Zhin Yan: gymnast

2 **2.2 Watch the video up to 0.30 without sound and check your answers to Exercise 1.**

3 **2.2 Watch the whole video with sound. Put the events in order.**
   1 Zhin Yan smiles on the roller coaster.
   2 She runs in the park.
   3 She visits the doctor.
   4 She shows us her bedroom.
   5 She walks into the school.
   6 She practises in her room.

4 **2.2 Watch the video up to 1.27 and complete the paragraph about Zhin Yan.**
   Zhin Yan is ¹.... years old. She goes to a special gymnastics ²..... She lives in Beijing, but she doesn't live with her ³..... She studies gymnastics ⁴.... days a week, ⁵.... hours a day. Once a week, the ⁶.... visits to check she's healthy.

5 **2.2 Watch the second part of the video (from 1.28). Are the sentences true (T) or false (F)? Correct the false ones.**
   1 On Saturday afternoons, Zhin Yan's mother visits her.
   2 Zhin Yan loves roller coasters.
   3 She always walks in the park.
   4 She goes back to school on Saturday evening.
   5 She gets up at 8 o'clock on Sunday.

Your turn

6 **Make a list of ways that Zhin Yan's life is different from yours. Use the ideas in Exercise 4 to help you.**

   Zhin Yan   Me
   She doesn't live with her parents.   I live with my parents.
   She sleeps at her school.
   She gets up at ...   I ...

7 **Work with a partner. Ask and answer questions using your notes.**

   Do you live with your parents?   Yes, I do.

26

Reading A blog

1 🔊 1.25 Look at the pictures. Where does the boy come from? What do you think he does in his free time? Read the blog and check your answers.

Hello from Bogotá!

SCHOOL OF THE MONTH

Hi, my name is Paco and I'm from Bogotá in Colombia. I'm eleven years old and I go to San Cristóbal Secondary School. Bogotá is the capital of Colombia, and over 7 million people live there. Colombia has a population of 47 million. We speak Spanish here.

I get up at 5.30 in the morning and have a shower. Then I have breakfast with my family. I've got one brother and one sister. My brother is sixteen and he goes to the same school as me. My sister is nineteen. School starts at 7.30, so I leave my house at 6.30. I always walk to school.

We study in the morning and break time is at 9.30. I love break times! I usually play football with my friends then.

I don't have lunch at school because school finishes at 11.30. That's when I go to the park with my friends to play football again! My mum comes to the park and walks home with me.

We have lunch at 1.30 at home. I love Colombian food – my mum cooks really good *arepas* – corn bread. We eat them with soup or meat. We have mango juice too – my favourite!

What do you do on a schoolday? Please tell me!

2 Read the blog again and answer the questions.
1. How old is Paco?
2. What time does he get up in the morning?
3. Where does he have lunch?

3 Find these numbers in the text. What do they mean?
a) 7,000,000   b) 16   c) 47,000,000   d) 19

Explore expressions with *have* 1

4 Read the article again. Find three phrases with *have* in the reading text.

5 Complete the sentences with *have* and the words below.

> a shower   a snack   dinner   a drink

1. I …. at 7.30 then I go to school.
2. I …. with my parents at 7 pm.
3. My brother …. when he comes out of school.
4. When I'm hot, I …. a …. .

➡ Vocabulary bank • page 108

Your turn

6 Work with a partner. One of you is Paco. Ask and answer the questions.
1. How many people live in your city?
2. When does school start in your country?
3. What do you do in your break time?
4. Do you eat lunch at school?
5. When does school finish?

> How many people live in your city?
>
> 7 million.

7 Compare Zhin Yan and Paco's lives. Write sentences.

Zhin Yan's schoolday starts at… but Paco's…

Speaking Asking for information

Real Talk: What do you do after school?

1 ▶ 2.3 Watch the teenagers in the video. Tick the activities you hear.
- play chess
- dance
- play tennis
- do homework
- read a book
- have art classes
- watch TV
- play video games
- go swimming
- do karate
- play the violin
- do drama
- play basketball

2 What do *you* do after school? Ask and answer with your partner.

5 🔊 1.26 Listen again and check your answers.

6 Work with a partner. Practise the conversation in Exercise 4.

7 Change the words in bold in the conversation in Exercise 4. Use the information below. Practise the conversation.

3 🔊 1.26 Listen to the conversation. What sport does Tom do?

4 Complete the conversation with the useful language.

Useful language

Do you know about …?
What days are the classes?
What time is the class?
How much does it cost?
Meet me

Tom:	Hi. Are you lost?
Gemma:	Yes, I am. I'm new at this school. …. **karate classes**?
Tom:	Yes, sure! I **do karate**. It isn't on today.
Gemma:	Oh! …. ?
Tom:	We have a class on **Wednesdays**.
Gemma:	OK. And …. ?
Tom:	It's from **7 pm to 8.30 pm**.
Gemma:	…. ?
Tom:	It's **£20** a month.
Gemma:	I'd really like to come. Can I come with you?
Tom:	Yes, of course you can! …. at the sports centre at **6.45 on Wednesday**.

WHAT'S ON AT SOUTHDOWN SPORTS AND LEISURE CENTRE?

Gymnastics	Monday 5.30–6.30 pm	£12
Karate	Wednesday 5.30–6.45 pm	£20
Dance	Monday 6.30–7.30 pm	£15
Swimming	Thursday 6.15–7.15 pm	£18
Tennis	Friday 5.30–7.30 pm	£15

Writing A blog post

1 Look at the photo of Madison Finsey, 13, a champion swimmer, and read her blog. Do you think her daily routine is easy or difficult?

Madison Finsey – CHAMPION SWIMMER

> Hi Madison! My question is: What's your routine before a competition?
> *Chloe*

Ask me a question!

> Hi Chloe
> I always get up at 6.45 and I have a big breakfast. I start school at 8.00 and finish at 2.15. I usually have lunch with the other swimmers. I swim in the pool and do exercises for four hours in the afternoon. I always get home about 7.30. After dinner, I do my homework. I haven't got a lot of free time, but I sometimes watch TV or chat online with my friends. Then I go to bed at 10.30. At the weekend, I go to the pool for six hours.

2 Cover Madison's blog in Exercise 1. What does she do at these times?

6.45 am	2.15 pm	10.30 pm
8.00 am	7.30 pm	

3 What time do you do the things in Exercise 2?

Useful language

Connectors
- Use *and* and *but* to put two ideas together in a sentence.
- Use *and* when one thing happens after another.
  I get up and I have a big breakfast.
- Use *but* when you contrast two ideas.
  I haven't got a lot of free time, but I sometimes watch TV.

4 Find examples of *and* and *but* in the text in Exercise 1.

5 Complete the sentences with *and* or *but*.
1 I get up .... have a shower.
2 I get up at 6.30 in the week .... at the weekend, I get up at 8.00.
3 I have lunch at school .... I don't like it.
4 I do my homework .... then I go to bed.
5 I like chocolate .... my sister doesn't.

Get Writing

PLAN

6 Make notes about your daily routine. Include information from Exercise 2.

WRITE

7 Write a blog post about your daily routine. Use your notes and the language below.

What
I get up / start school … /
When
… at 8.30. / In the morning … / On Wednesdays … / After school …
How often
I always / usually / often / sometimes …

CHECK

8 Can you say YES to these questions?
- Have you got examples of connectors in your blog?
- Is the information in your blog in chronological (time) order?
- Are your spelling, grammar and vocabulary correct?

1–2 Review

Vocabulary

1 Complete the sentences with the words in the box.

> cousin   grandma   classmate   ~~aunt~~
> granddad   uncle   parents

1 Your mum's sister is your *aunt*.
2 Your dad's dad is your ….
3 Your aunt's daughter is your ….
4 Your dad's brother is your ….
5 Your mum's mum is your ….
6 A student in your class is your ….
7 Your mum and dad are your ….

2 Choose the correct words to describe the pictures.

My brother is ¹**tall** / **short**. His hair is ²**spiky** / **curly** and ³**dark** / **fair**. His eyes are big and ⁴**brown** / **blue**.

My sister is ⁵**short** / **tall**. Her hair is ⁶**short** / **long** and ⁷**brown** / **red**. Her eyes are ⁸**green** / **brown**.

3 Write the phrase for each picture.

1 *get up*

4 Complete the after school activities.

1 *music*

1 do …

2 go …

3 have … classes

4 play …

5 play …

6 have … classes

Explore vocabulary

5 Complete the sentences with the adjectives in the box.

> big   happy   ~~lucky~~   wonderful
> colourful   good   noisy

1 I'm very *lucky* because I've got four sisters.
2 You're very …. Be quiet!
3 She likes …. clothes in the summer – especially yellow, orange, and green.
4 Thank you for this …. meal. I love it!
5 Steven isn't a bad boy – he's a …. boy.
6 There are nine people in my family, so we live in a …. house.
7 We're …. because we haven't got school today.

6 Complete the text. Choose the correct preposition of time, and write the correct form of *have*.

I usually get up ¹ **at** / **in** 7.30 ² **at** / **in** the morning and ³ …. a shower. Then we all ⁴ …. breakfast. At school, I ⁵ …. lunch ⁶ **at** / **in** 1 o'clock. My sister sometimes ⁷ …. a snack ⁸ **at** / **in** the afternoon, but I usually just ⁹ …. a drink ¹⁰ **at** / **in** that time. ¹¹ **At** / **In** night we all ¹² …. dinner quite late, and then go to bed.

30

Language focus

1 Look at the pictures. Complete the sentences with the correct form of *have got*.

 I ¹ *'ve got* (✓) two avatars. One avatar is Esmeralda. She ² .... (✓) green hair. She ³ .... (✗) green eyes, she ⁴ .... (✓) blue eyes. My second avatar is RocketBoy. He ⁵ .... (✓) purple hair. He ⁶ .... (✗) blue eyes, he ⁷ .... (✓) green eyes. In real life, I ⁸ .... (✓) a sister and a brother. They ⁹ .... (✗) green hair! They ¹⁰ .... (✓) brown hair, like me.

2 Put the words in the correct order.

1 *I have got three sisters.*

1. got / have / three / sisters / I
2. haven't / I / a brother / got
3. a big house / Have / got / you?
4. got / My grandmother / an old car / has
5. James / a dog / Has / got?
6. bicycles / got / have / All my friends
7. got / haven't / We / a computer

3 Complete the conversation.

1. A: My dad is **tall**.
   B: My dad *is taller than* your dad!
2. A: Our house is **big**.
   B: Our house .... your house!
3. A: My grandparents are **young**.
   B: My grandparents .... your grandparents!
4. A: My uncle is **funny**.
   B: My aunt .... your uncle!
5. A: I'm very **intelligent**.
   B: My baby sister .... you!
6. A: I'm a **good** singer.
   B: I .... you!

4 Complete the text about Luis's cousin. Use the correct form of the verbs in brackets.

My cousin Alex ¹ *lives* (live) in England. English school children ² .... (have) a different daily routine. A typical school day ³ .... (start) between 8.30 and 9.00. Pupils ⁴ .... (not have) lunch at home, they ⁵ .... (eat) at school. In my country, we ⁶ .... (not eat) at school. They ⁷ .... (finish) school at about 3.30. We ⁸ .... (finish) at 2.00. My cousin usually ⁹ .... (have) dinner at about 5.00. Finally, he ¹⁰ .... (go) to bed at about 9.30. I think that's very early! I ¹¹ .... (not go) to bed until about 11.00!

UNIT 1–2

5 Complete the questions about the text in Exercise 3 with *do* or *does*.

1. *Does* Alex live in Spain?
2. What time .... English school children start school?
3. Where .... English school children have lunch?
4. .... children at Alex's school finish at 3:30?
5. What time .... Luis finish school?
6. .... Alex go to bed before Luis?

6 Write the words in the correct order.

1 *I always play tennis at the weekend.*

1. always / I / tennis / play / at the weekend
2. sometimes / I / am / late for school
3. watches / TV in her bedroom / Rosie / never
4. happy on Saturdays / She / usually / is
5. after school / often / play football / They
6. in her bedroom / is / My sister / always

Language builder

7 Choose the correct words to complete the conversation.

A: Hi Rosie. Hey, you ¹ **'ve / 's** got new rollerblades! They look great.
B: Thanks. They're ² **better / gooder** than my old pair. They're ³ **expensiver / more expensive**, too! ⁴ **Have you got / Have got you** rollerblades?
A: No, I ⁵ **hasn't / haven't**. My sister ⁶ **has / have** got a pair, and she ⁷ **love / loves** them. But I ⁸ **like / likes** skateboarding.
B: Really? How often ⁹ **do / does** you go skateboarding?
A: I ¹⁰ **never / usually** go to the skate park on Saturdays with my cousin. What about you? ¹¹ **Who / What** do you go rollerblading with? ¹² **Do you / Are you** go with your brother?
B: No, I ¹³ **don't / 'm not**. I ¹⁴ **never / sometimes** go with him! He ¹⁵ **don't / doesn't** like rollerblading.

Speaking

8 Match the sentence pairs.

1. Hello.
2. How are you?
3. How much does this cost?
4. What day is the dance class?
5. Have you got Olivia's phone number?
6. What time is the class?
7. Can I call you back?

a) Hi, it's Steve.
b) Sure. Talk to you later.
c) From 5pm to 6.30pm.
d) It's £15.
e) Fine, thanks.
f) It's on Thursdays.
g) Yes, it's 980390.

3 Schooldays

Discovery EDUCATION

In this unit ...

Kung Fu school **p35**

South African schoolgirl **p38**

Using your phone at school **p40**

CLIL Da Vinci's design **p117**

Vocabulary
- Places in school
- School subjects
- Nouns and verbs
- Adjectives

Grammar
- *can* for ability and permission
- Object pronouns
- like/love/hate/don't mind + ing

Unit aims
I can ...
- describe my school and school subjects.
- talk about what I like and don't like.
- understand about schools in other countries.
- talk about things we can and can't do.
- ask and answer questions about personal information.
- write an email about my school.

BE CURIOUS
What can you see in the photo?
Start thinking
- What country is it?
- Who are the children?
- Where are they going?

Vocabulary Places in a school

1 Look at the plan of a secondary school. Which places have you got in your school?

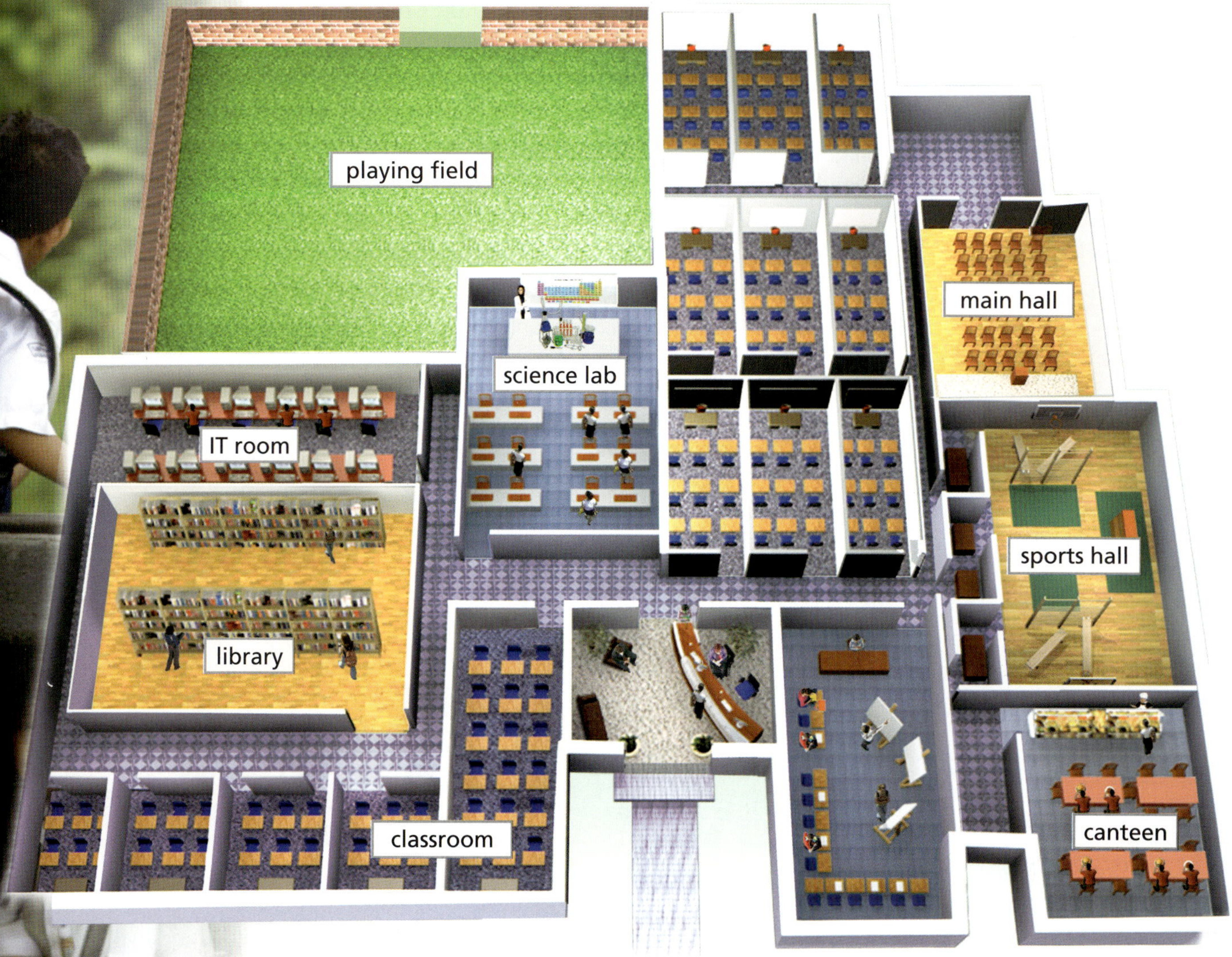

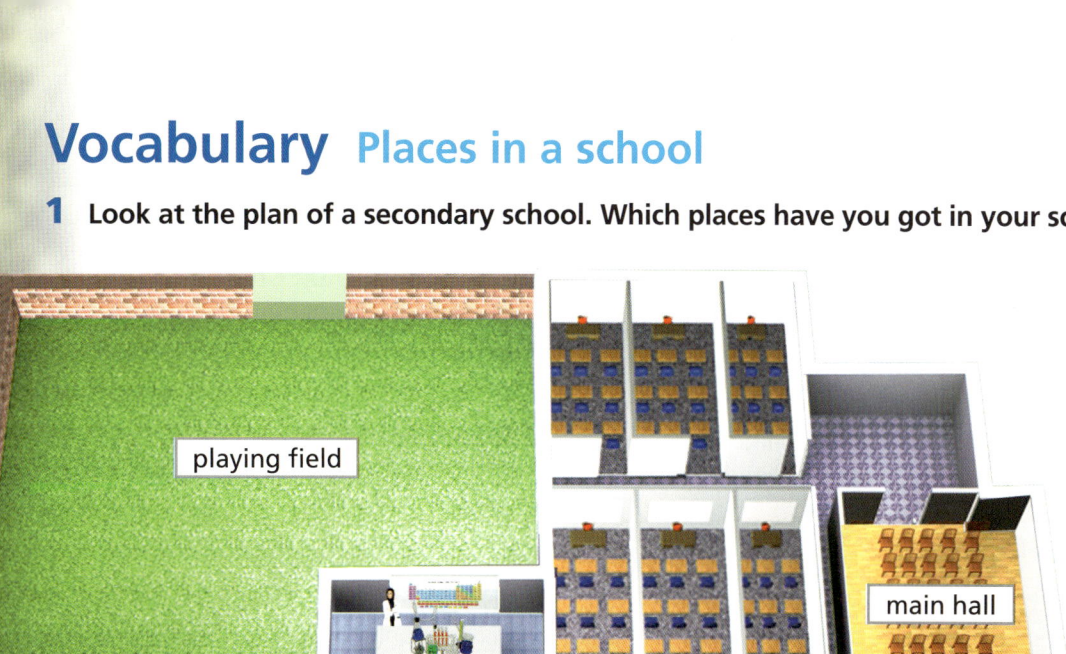

2 🔊 1.27 Match the sentences 1–8 with the places in Exercise 1. Then listen, check and repeat.
1. We have lunch here. *canteen*
2. The whole school meets here.
3. We do outdoor sports here.
4. This is where we do indoor sports and exercise.
5. We work with computers in this room.
6. This is where we do experiments.
7. We read and study here.
8. This is where our main lessons are.

Your turn

3 Draw a map of a school. Write the names of the places.

4 Use the map to ask and answer questions about the school.

> This school is very big. This is the sports hall, and this is the main hall.

> What's this?

> It's the science lab. It's got …

➡ **Vocabulary bank • page 109**

33

KUNG FU SCHOOL

DRAGON

SNAKE

FROG

Kung Fu is a 'martial art'. It's also a great Chinese tradition. Chinese children can go to special schools and study Kung Fu every day!

After they finish their studies, the students can get good jobs in the army or the police force.

Li Zheng, from Shanghai, is thirteen years old. She practises Kung Fu in the playing field every day with hundreds of other students. She wants to be a police officer in the future. Every morning and evening, Li does her exercises and practises her Kung Fu moves and positions for hours. The training is difficult and Li can't live at home. She can only see her family in the holidays. Li can do a lot of different moves like the frog, the dragon and the snake. Her teacher is an expert in Kung Fu. He can break a brick with his hand! Can Li break a brick with her hands? No, she can't!

FACT! Some martial arts are at least two thousand years old!

Reading A magazine article

1. 🔊 1.28 Look at the title and pictures. Where is the school, do you think? Why do you think the students are there? How old is the girl in the picture?

2. Read the text again. Are the sentences true (*T*) or false (*F*)? Correct the false ones.
   1. Li Zheng practises Kung Fu with other people. *T*
   2. Li Zheng lives at home.
   3. Li Zheng wants to work in a school.
   4. Li Zheng doesn't see her parents very often.

3. Answer the questions.
   1. What does she want to do in the future?
   2. When does she see her parents?

Explore nouns and verbs

4. Find the verbs and nouns in the article. Copy and complete the table. Then complete the sentences.

Verb	Noun
a study	….
b ….	practice
c train	….
d exercise	….

1. There are a lot of grammar …. in this book.
2. I get up at 6 o'clock every day and …. the piano.
3. After I finish my …. , I want to go to university.
4. My sister wants to be a teacher. She's at teacher …. college.

➡ **Vocabulary bank** • page 109

Your turn

5. Ask and answer the questions.
   1. Would you like to go to Li Zheng's school? Why/Why not?
   2. Would you like to learn a martial art? Why/Why not?

Language focus 1
can for ability and permission

1 Complete the examples from the text on page 34.

	I / You / He / She / It / We / They
+	He .... **break** a brick with his hand! Chinese children .... to special schools and **study** Kung Fu every day!
−	Li .... live at home. They **can't** see their parents during the week.
?	.... Li **break** a brick with her hands? Yes, she **can**. / No, she .... . **Can** they **break** a brick with their hands? Yes, they **can**. / No, they **can't**.

 Grammar reference • page 101

Get it right!
Notice that *can* doesn't change in the third person.
I can play guitar.
He can play the guitar.
~~He cans play the guitar~~ ✗

2 Write sentences with *I can* and *I can't*. Use the ideas below and add your own ideas.
- do a handstand
- write an email in English
- do Kung Fu
- ride a bike
- play football
- play the guitar
- speak French
- swim 50 metres

I can ride a bike.
I can't speak French ...

Say it right!

a 🔊 **1.29** Listen and choose the option you hear.

I can't
1 I **can / can't** hear you.
2 She **can / can't** come for dinner.
3 Pablo **can / can't** help you with your homework.
4 They **can / can't** count to 20 in French.
5 **Can / Can't** you wear jeans at school?

b 🔊 **1.29** Listen and repeat the sentences.

Your turn

3 Work with a partner. Ask and answer the questions in Exercise 2.

Can you do a handstand?

No, I can't. Can you ...?

4 Write sentences about your partner's abilities.
Marta can ride a bike but she can't ...

5 Write about things you can and can't do at home and at school. Use the ideas below and your own ideas.
- use my mobile phone in the classroom
- go to bed late on school nights
- wear what I want at home
- talk in class
- go to bed late at weekends

I can't use my mobile phone in the classroom but I can ...

6 Work with a partner. Ask and answer questions about the information in Exercise 5.

Can you talk in class?

Yes, we can!

Learn about a different Kung Fu school in China.
- What do students learn at the school?
- How many boys study at the school?
- What do the students learn how to do at the school?

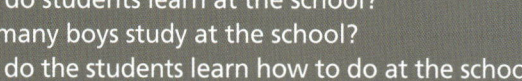
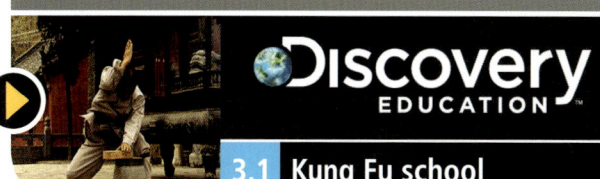

3.1 Kung Fu school

Listening A podcast

1 Look at the New Bank School website. How is it different from your school?

2 🔊 1.30 Listen to Tom talking about the school. What's his favourite lesson?

3 🔊 1.30 Listen again. Complete the information.

1 *great*

1. Tom thinks his teachers are …
2. The school day starts at 9 am and finishes at …
3. They have three lessons in the morning and … lessons in the afternoon.
4. On Saturday, they only have lessons in the …
5. Tom wants to be a professional … when he leaves school.

Vocabulary School subjects

4 🔊 1.31 Match the school subjects in the box with the pictures (a–i). Then listen, check and repeat.

a *History*

> Science   Geography   Maths   ICT
> PE   ~~History~~   French   English   Music

  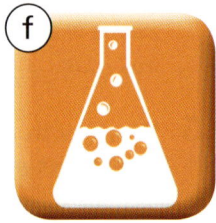

➡ **Vocabulary bank** • page 109

THE NEW BANK
SCHOOL OF PERFORMING ARTS
TRAINING PERFORMERS FOR THE FUTURE!

HOME   ABOUT   EVENTS

Click *here* and listen to Tom talking about his life at New Bank.

Your turn

5 Complete the sentences for you. Then work with a partner. Ask and answer questions.

My favourite subjects are   *Maths and Science*
I don't like …
I don't study …
I'm good at …

> What are your favourite subjects?

> Maths and Science. What about you?

6 Write sentences about you and your partner.

My favourite subjects are … I don't like …
I'm good at … My partner likes …

Language focus 2 Object pronouns

1 Complete the examples from the listening on page 36.
1. That's .... in the blue shorts!
2. It's a really good school and I love ....!
3. I like .... but I prefer Dance.
4. I practise with .... on Saturday afternoons.
5. Our teachers tell .... it's really important to do our academic schoolwork.

2 Match the object pronouns in the box with the subject pronouns.

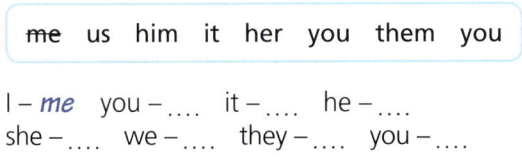

~~me~~ us him it her you them you

I – *me*   you – ....   it – ....   he – ....
she – ....   we – ....   they – ....   you – ....

→ Grammar reference • page 101

(don't) like, don't mind, love, hate + ing

3 Look at the sentences from the listening on page 36. What do you notice about the form of the second verb in a–c?
a) I don't mind working this hard.
b) I *really* don't like getting up early on Saturday mornings!
c) I love dancing.
d) I like the lessons, but I'm really tired at the end of the week.

Use verbs ending in *-ing* after (*don't*) *like*, *don't mind*, *love*, and *hate*					
😍	🙂	😐	🙁	😫
love	like	don't mind	don't like	hate

→ Grammar reference • page 101

4 Write complete sentences that are true for you.
1. I / watch / sport on TV.
   I love watching sport on TV.
2. My best friend / play / computer games.
3. I do / my homework.
4. My teacher / stay / up late at weekends.
5. My friends / go / to the cinema.

5 Read the quiz. Choose the correct answers for you. Write one more example for each section.

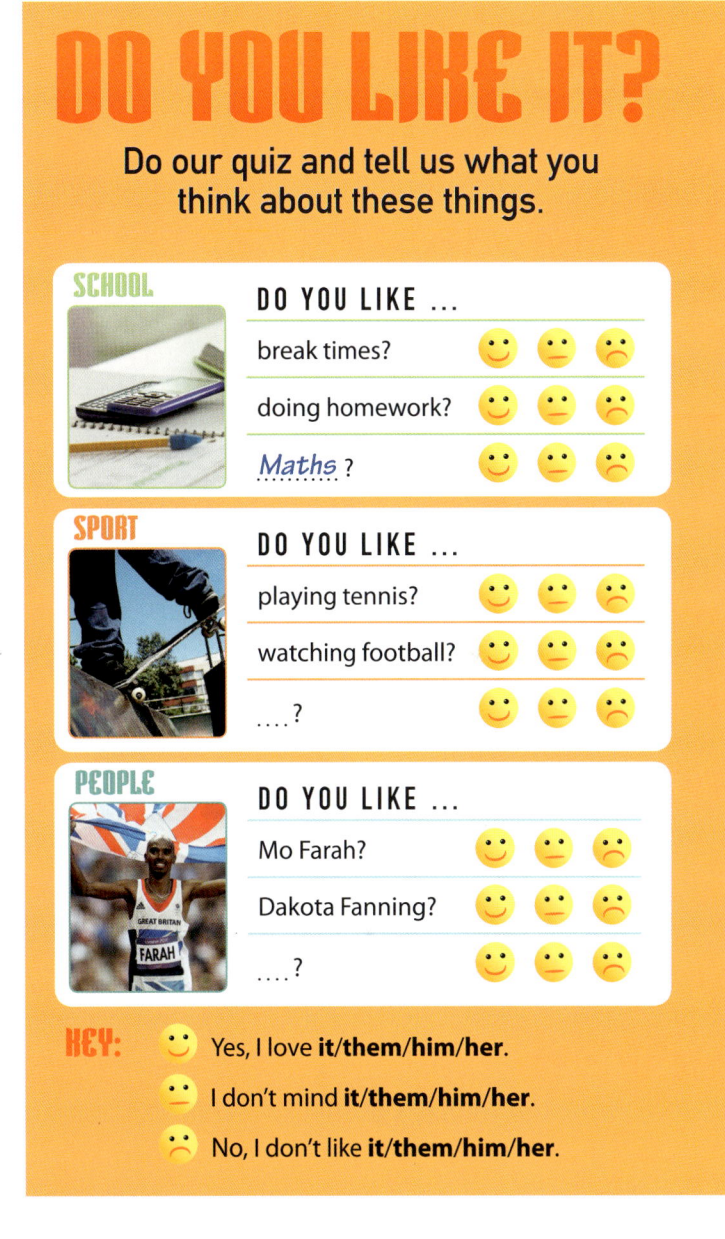

DO YOU LIKE IT?

Do our quiz and tell us what you think about these things.

SCHOOL

DO YOU LIKE …
- break times?   🙂 😐 🙁
- doing homework?   🙂 😐 🙁
- *Maths* ?   🙂 😐 🙁

SPORT

DO YOU LIKE …
- playing tennis?   🙂 😐 🙁
- watching football?   🙂 😐 🙁
- …. ?   🙂 😐 🙁

PEOPLE

DO YOU LIKE …
- Mo Farah?   🙂 😐 🙁
- Dakota Fanning?   🙂 😐 🙁
- …. ?   🙂 😐 🙁

KEY:
🙂 Yes, I love **it/them/him/her**.
😐 I don't mind **it/them/him/her**.
🙁 No, I don't like **it/them/him/her**.

Your turn

6 Work with a partner. Ask and answer the questions in the quiz. Use the phrases in the key.

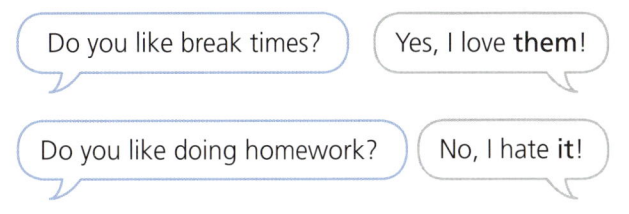

— Do you like break times?
— Yes, I love **them**!

— Do you like doing homework?
— No, I hate **it**!

7 Write sentences from Exercise 6. Use object pronouns.
I hate doing homework but my partner doesn't mind it.

Discover Culture

1 **Look at the map and the picture. Who is the man in the photo? Where was he from?**

2 **Look at the pictures of Tobilay and answer the questions.**
   1 Where is she?
   2 How old is she?
   3 Where is she from?

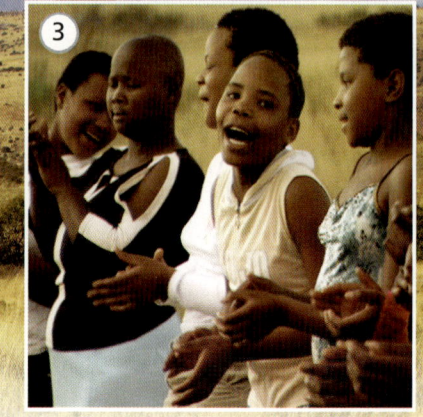

Find out about a school in South Africa.

Discovery EDUCATION

3.2 South African schoolgirl

3 **3.2 Watch the video up to 0.38 and check your answers to Exercise 2.**

4 **Are the sentences true (T) or false (F)? Correct the false ones.**
   1 The school children wear white shirts.
   2 They have pasta for lunch.
   3 The children sing and dance in a field.
   4 Both boys and girls play netball.
   5 Tobilay does her homework at school.

5 **3.2 Watch the video again and complete Tobilay's profile.**

Tobilay is ¹.... years old. She walks ².... kilometres to school every morning. School starts at ³.... o'clock. Every morning she ⁴.... the national song with her classmates. In the afternoon she studies Zulu ⁵.... and learns traditional South African ⁶.... and ⁷..... She loves ⁸....! In the evening she does her ⁹...., writes in her ¹⁰...., and reads her ¹¹.... from class. This evening she's got a lot of ¹²....!

6 **Look at the pictures. Complete the captions about South African culture.**
   a) Today it's Nelson Mandela's .....
   b) The national anthem has words from .... different South African languages.
   c) They learn traditional South African .... and .....

7 **3.2 Watch the video again to check your answers to Exercise 6.**

Your turn

8 **Work with a partner. Compare your school day to Tobilay's school day. Use the topics below.**
   - How I get to school
   - Time my school starts
   - Activities I do in the morning
   - Activities I do in the afternoon
   - Homework

Tobilay walks to school but I go to school by car. What about you?

9 **Write a description of your usual day at school. Compare it to Tobilay's.**

I don't walk to school, I go by bus.
Our school doesn't start at 8am, it starts at 8.30 am.

UNIT 3

Reading A profile

1 🔊 1.32 Look at the map and photos. Where's Wales? What extra activities do you think students do in Wales? Read Gareth's blog and check your answers.

2 🔊 1.33 Read the profile again and complete the sentences about Gareth and his friends. Listen and check.

1. Gareth speaks two languages, …. and …. . He speaks …. with his family. He goes to the …. club. He can …. . He loves …. .
2. Isabel goes to the …. club. She loves …. .
3. Darren goes to the …. club. He can …. .

Explore adjectives

3 Find these adjectives in the text. Which ones mean 'very good'? Which one means 'very bad'?

a) interesting
b) great
c) boring
d) brilliant
e) terrible
f) fast
g) slow

4 Find the opposites for these adjectives in Exercise 3.

a) interesting _boring_
b) brilliant ….
c) fast ….

➡ **Vocabulary bank** • page 109

A Welsh school

Hi! My name's Gareth and I'm a student at Penglais Comprehensive School in Aberystwyth, a small town in Wales. In my school we study both English and Welsh. At home, Welsh is our first language so I usually speak Welsh with my parents and grandparents. I like listening to my grandfather tell interesting stories in Welsh.

Our school is great because we've got lots of different clubs.

There's a guitar club on Thursdays. Students can learn how to play the guitar. My friend Isabel goes to this club. She really loves playing music and singing and she's really good. I'm terrible at singing!

We also have a hip-hop group. Students can learn hip-hop music and dance and sometimes they have concerts.

My friend Darren goes to Rugby Club. He can run very fast but I'm really slow! Lots of Welsh people love playing and watching rugby but I think it's boring!

I go to Surf Club every Tuesday after school. We can surf and swim. I love surfing and I can swim fast. Our teacher is an expert surfer. He's brilliant but he shouts a lot!

FACT! The Welsh alphabet doesn't have the letters K, Q, V or Z.

Your turn

5 Compare your school with Tobilay's and Gareth's schools. Copy and complete the chart.

	Tobilay's school	Gareth's school	My school
Languages			
Activities / Clubs			
Likes / Loves			

6 Write sentences. Then work with a partner and compare your sentences.

In Tobilay's school they speak a lot of languages.
In Gareth's school they speak … In my school …

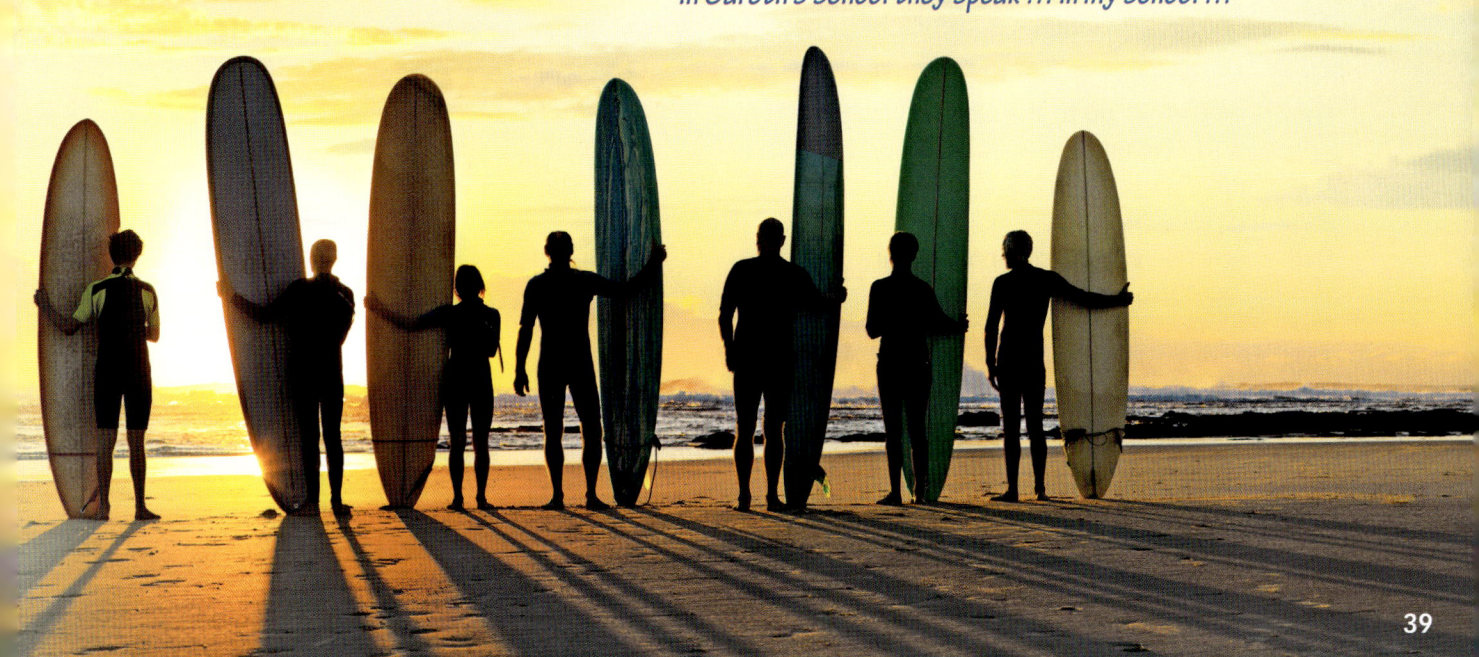

Speaking Asking and giving permission

Real Talk: Can you use your mobile phone at school?

1 ▶ 3.3 Watch the teenagers in the video. How many of the teenagers …

a) can use their phones anywhere in school?
b) can only use their phones in class to surf the internet?
c) can't use their phones anywhere in school?

2 💬 Can *you* use your mobile phone at school? Ask and answer with your partner.

5 🔊 1.34 Listen again and check your answers.

6 💬 Work with a partner. Practise the conversation in Exercise 4.

7 💬 Change the words in bold in the conversation in Exercise 4. Use the information below. Practise the conversation.

You want to …
… have breakfast in bed
… borrow £10
… wear your new trainers to school
… go swimming on Sunday afternoon.

> Mum, can I have breakfast in bed?

> No, sorry …

3 🔊 1.34 Listen to the conversation. When can Fran and Bella go to the cinema?

4 Complete the conversation with the useful language.

Useful language

Great, thanks …   Why not?   Yes, you can.
Can I / we …?   … sorry, I'm afraid you can't.

Fran:	Hi Dad. …. **go to the cinema** with Bella this **evening**?
Dad:	No, …. .
Fran:	…. ?
Dad:	Because **your uncle and aunt are here this evening**.
Fran:	…. go on **Saturday** then, please?
Dad:	…. .
Fran:	…. , Dad!

40

Writing An email

UNIT 3

Hi,
Please send me an email with information about your school for my school project. Thanks!
Günter ▶

Hey Günter,
Here's some info about my school for your project. I go to Humphrey Davy School in Penzance, England. It's a big school! It's got about 50 teachers and 900 pupils, from 11 to 16 years old. We have six classes in each year, with about 30 pupils in each class. We have a school uniform ☹. You can see it in the photo (we can't wear jeans or trainers). The school day starts at 9 o'clock and finishes at 3.30 pm.

In my year, we study a lot of subjects – 12!!! ☹. My favourite subject's Maths. Every teacher's got a different room, so we go to a different classroom every lesson. All the classrooms are big and we have posters on the walls with our projects ☺.

That's all for now. Write back if you need more info! Bye!
Anna ▶

1 Read Anna's reply to Günter. Where's her school? How many pupils are there?

2 Answer questions about Anna's school.
1. What's the name of the school?
2. Is it big or small?
3. How old are the pupils?
4. Do they have a uniform?
5. What time does school start and finish?
6. How many subjects does Anna do?
7. What's her favourite subject?

3 Find examples of informal language in Anna's email.

Useful language

Informal language
In an email to a friend, use informal language …
- to start: *Hi, …*.
- to end: *That's all for now. Bye!* ….
- contractions: *Here's* …., …. …. …. ….
- abbreviations: *info*

4 Complete the Useful language box with the phrases below.

| Hello!   Bye for now!   How are you?   How's it going? |

5 Make these sentences informal. Use the Useful language box to help you.
1. Dear Anna,
2. My class teacher is great.
3. My school is very big – it has got 1,500 pupils.
4. We have got a new teacher.
5. Best wishes, Günter

Get Writing

PLAN

6 Make notes about your school. Include information from Exercise 2.
- The name of your school
- The size (big, small?)
- Pupils' age
- Uniform?
- Time school starts and finishes
- Subjects

WRITE

7 Write an email to Günter. Use your notes and the language below.

*I go to …
It's a … school with …
The pupils are …
We have / haven't got …
The school day …
The classrooms are …*

CHECK

8 Can you say YES to these questions?
- Have you got information from Exercise 6 in your email?
- Have you got informal language?
- Are your spelling, grammar and punctuation correct?

4 Food!

Discovery EDUCATION

In this unit ...

Fishing in Japan **p45**

Dabbawallas **p48**

Your lunch **p50**

CLIL Mountains of rice **p118**

Vocabulary
- Food
- Snacks and takeaways
- Meals and courses
- Expressions with *have* 2
- International words

Language focus
- Countable and uncountable nouns
- *a/an, some/any*
- *There is/are*
- *much/many/a lot of*

Unit aims
I can ...
- identify different kinds of food.
- use simple expressions with *have*.
- talk about meals and courses.
- talk about countable and uncountable nouns.
- understand about food in the UK and other countries.
- order food and drink in a restaurant.
- write a report about a celebration.
- use basic time connectors.

BE CURIOUS

What can you see in the photo?
Start thinking
- How many of the foods in the picture can you name?
- Which are healthy?
- Which ones do you like/dislike?

Vocabulary Food

1 🔊 1.35 Look at the picture. Match the pictures with the food and drink words in the box. Then listen, check and repeat.

.... apples   .... banana   _1_ beans   .... bread   .... butter   .... carrot   .... cheese
.... chicken   .... eggs   .... fish   .... pizza   .... pasta   .... rice   .... meat   .... milk

2 Copy and complete the table. Which food in the pictures is healthy? Which is not very healthy?

Dairy	Fruit	Vegetables	Meat and fish	Other
cheese				_bread_

Your turn

3 Ask and answer questions about the food you like and don't like. Write your partner's answers.

> Do you like beans?

> Yes, I do. Do you like …?

4 Work in small groups. Tell your friends about your partner.

> Ana likes … but she doesn't like …

➡ Vocabulary bank • page 110

LUNCHES AROUND THE WORLD!

A Simon is from England. He takes a packed lunch to school. In his lunch box there are usually two sandwiches, some fruit, a chocolate bar and some juice. In the summer, Simon eats his lunch with his friends in the playground. Today, Simon has got some cheese sandwiches, an orange and some apple juice, but he says, 'I'm not happy because I haven't got a chocolate bar!'

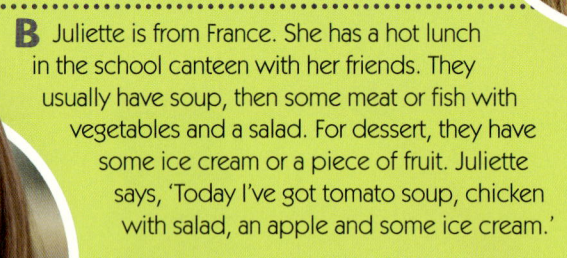

B Juliette is from France. She has a hot lunch in the school canteen with her friends. They usually have soup, then some meat or fish with vegetables and a salad. For dessert, they have some ice cream or a piece of fruit. Juliette says, 'Today I've got tomato soup, chicken with salad, an apple and some ice cream.'

C Kazuyo is from Japan. She takes a Bento Box to school. In it there is usually some rice, vegetables and fish or meat. It's healthy and fun. Japanese parents make the rice into different shapes: popular cartoon characters, animals, flowers and buildings! The children have fun eating them. Kazuyo says, 'I've got some rice and some fish, but I haven't got any meat today. My rice is in the shape of a panda. It's really cute!'

Reading A magazine article

1 Look at the photos. What food can you see?

2 🔊 1.36 Read the article about school lunches. Match the people with their lunches.

3 Read the article again. Choose the correct answers.
   1. There are **sandwiches / vegetables and fish** in a Bento Box.
   2. Simon **usually has / never has** chocolate in his lunch box.
   3. Juliette **usually has / never has** soup for lunch.
   4. There is **some / isn't any** chocolate in Simon's lunchbox today.
   5. The food in Bento Boxes is unusual because it's **fun to eat / unhealthy**.
   6. Juliette eats with her friends in the school **playground / canteen**.

Explore expressions with *have* 2

4 Read the article again. Find two phrases with *have*.

5 Complete the sentences with the words below.

   lunch   problem   fun

   1. We always have .... in the canteen at 1 o'clock.
   2. I usually have .... when I'm with my friends.
   3. Do you have a .... with this exercise?

➔ **Vocabulary bank** • page 110

Your turn

6 Work with a partner. Ask and answer the questions.
   1. Where do you usually have your lunch?
   2. Do you have a school lunch or a packed lunch?
   3. Who makes your lunch?

Language focus 1 Countable and uncountable nouns

1 Complete the examples from the text on page 44.

Countable nouns	Uncountable nouns
two sandwiches, an orange, a .... , an	fruit, rice, ... , ...

➜ Grammar reference • page 102

2 Copy and complete the table. Which words are countable and which are uncountable? Add some more words.

> ~~banana~~ meat   milk   ~~ice cream~~   vegetables
> water   cheese   sandwich   carrots   apple

countable	uncountable
banana	ice cream

a/an, some and any

3 Complete the examples from the text on page 44.

Singular countable
I've got **an** orange.
I haven't got .... chocolate bar.
Have you got .... orange?

Plural countable
I've got **some** sandwiches.
I haven't got **any** sandwiches.
Have you got **any** sandwiches?

Uncountable
I've got **some** rice.
I haven't got .... meat.
Have you got .... rice?

➜ Grammar reference • page 102

4 Circle the correct words.
1. I'm a vegetarian. I don't eat **some** / (**any**) meat.
2. Have you got **a** / **any** fruit in your lunch box?
3. I need **any** / **some** water – I'm really thirsty.
4. They haven't got **any** / **some** apples.
5. Do you eat **an** / **any** orange every day?
6. I've got **some** / **a** chocolate bar.

5 Read and match the texts with the correct fridge. Then complete the text with *a, an, some* or *any*.

1. Our fridge isn't very full. We've got [1].... egg, [2].... milk and [3].... cheese. We haven't got [4].... fish and we haven't got [5].... meat, but we've got [6].... vegetables.
2. In our fridge we've got [7].... big cake. We've got [8].... ice cream too, and [9].... drinks. We haven't got [10].... sandwiches. My brother doesn't like sandwiches. But we've got four big pizzas!

Your turn

6 Draw a fridge with five food and drink words from this unit.

7 Work with a partner. Ask and answer questions about what's in your fridges.

> Have you got any milk in your fridge?
> Yes, I have.
>
> Have you got any sandwiches?
> No, I haven't.

8 Draw your partner's fridge.

Learn about fishing in Japan.
- Which ocean is Japan in?
- Why is the sea so important to Japanese people?
- What do the women find in the sea?

4.1 Fishing in Japan

Listening A conversation

1 Look at the picture. Where are the teenagers? What do you think they are talking about?

2 🔊 1.37 Listen to the conversation between Tim and Michelle. Who has got food? What does Tim want?

3 🔊 1.37 Listen again. Are the sentences about Michelle (*M*) or Tim (*T*)?
1 … has got a packed lunch. M
2 … has got some money for presents. ….
3 … is hungry now. ….
4 … always has a big breakfast. ….
5 … asks for a sandwich. ….
6 … wants to buy a burger. ….
7 … has got £20. ….

Vocabulary Meals and courses

4 Copy and complete the table. Put the words from the listening into the correct column. There is one extra word. What is it?

> ~~breakfast~~   dessert   dinner   lunch
> main course   snack   starter

Meal	Courses (parts of a meal)
breakfast	….
….	….
….	….

5 🔊 1.38 Listen, check and repeat.

➡ **Vocabulary bank** • page 110

Your turn

6 Work with a partner. Ask and answer questions about meals.

> What time do you usually have breakfast?

> I usually have breakfast at 7.30.

> What do you have for a snack at school?

> I sometimes have …

Language focus 2
there is / there are

1 Complete the examples from the listening on page 46.
1. There .... a lot of cool places to eat in London.
2. .... there a fast food place near here?
3. .... there any sweets?
4. There .... a fast food place on the way home.
5. There .... a great fast food place on the way home.

➡ Grammar reference • page 102

2 Circle the correct option. Are the sentences true for your town and school?
1. There **is / are** a supermarket in my town.
2. There **isn't / aren't** any pizza places.
3. There **is / are** a sports centre in my town.
4. There **isn't / aren't** a café in my school.

3 Look at the picture. Complete the questions with *is* or *are*. Write some more questions.

1. .... there any fruit?
2. .... there any vegetables?
3. .... there any chocolate bars?
4. .... there any juice?

Say it right!
Intonation in questions

a When we ask *yes/no* questions in English, our voice goes up. In answers, our voice goes down.

Is there any pasta?   Yes, there is.

b Match the questions with the answers.
1. Are there any olives? a Yes, I do.
2. Is there a supermarket? b No, there aren't.
3. Do you like milkshakes? c Yes, there is.
4. Does he like oranges? d No, he doesn't.

c 🔊 1.39 Listen, check and repeat.

4 💬 Work with a partner. Ask and answer the questions in Exercise 3.

Is there any fruit?   Yes, there is.

UNIT 4

much / many / a lot of

5 Complete the examples from the listening on page 46.
1. There are .... cool places to eat.
2. I haven't got .... money.
3. How .... food have you got?
4. I've got .... food.
5. How .... sandwiches have you got?

➡ Grammar reference • page 102

6 Complete the sentences with the words below.

> How much   ~~How many~~   a lot of (x2)
> many   much

1. *How many* apples are there?
2. There are .... apples. 
3. There aren't .... apples.
4. .... water is there?
5. There isn't .... water.
6. There's .... water.

Your turn

7 What's in your bag? Write two things that you've got in your bag today. Try to use one countable and one uncountable thing.
I've got some pens.
I've got some water.

8 Work with a partner. Ask what's in his/her bag. Then ask *How much* or *How many*.

What have you got in your bag?

I've got some pens.

How many pens have you got?

Discover Culture

1. **Look at the map and picture 1. Where's Mumbai? What do you know about it?**

2. **Match the countries to the pictures (2–5). What food or drink do they deliver?**
   a) *2 - ice cream*

   a) The UK ....
   b) Italy ....
   c) Brazil ....
   d) Mexico ....

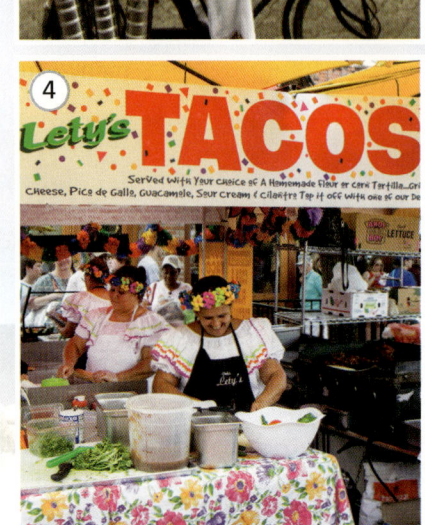

3. **Look at the picture of Arvind (1) and answer the questions.**
   1. What is his job?
   2. What food do you think he delivers?
   3. How does he do it?
   4. Is his job easy or difficult? Is it safe or dangerous?

Find out about lunches in Mumbai.

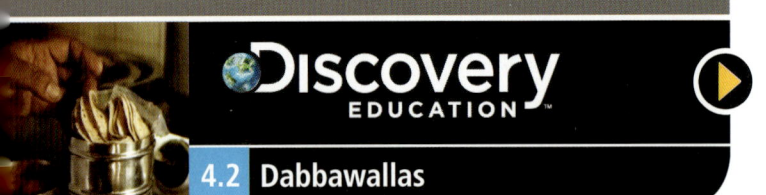

Discovery EDUCATION

4.2 Dabbawallas

4. ▶ 4.2 **Watch the video and check your answers to Exercise 3.**

5. ▶ 4.2 **Watch the video again. Are the sentences true (T) or false (F)? Correct the false ones.**
   1. The trains in Mumbai are very empty.
   2. The dabbawallas put the boxes into coloured bags.
   3. Then they put the boxes into a truck.
   4. They don't deliver the food by hand.

6. ▶ 4.2 **Watch the video again and complete the paragraph about Arvind.**
   Arvind is Aruna's ¹ *cousin* . He is a dabbawalla in Mumbai. He takes ² .... to people. The food goes in a ³ .... lunch box. There are ⁴ .... thousand dabbawallas in Mumbai, and they take lunches to ⁵ .... thousand people. It is a dangerous job because there is always a lot of ⁶ .... in the city.

7. **Test your memory. Which of these places do you see in the video?**

   kitchen   busy street   airport
   restaurant   station   office   beach

Your turn

8. **What kind of food deliveries or street food is there in your town?**
   In my town there are pizza deliveries.

9. **How often do you:**
   • eat street food?
   • get a takeaway?

   How often do you eat street food?

   Not very often. What about you?

TYPICAL ENGLISH FOOD

People all over the world say that English food is bad. Thirteen-year-old Rupa Remy doesn't agree. We interview her in her house in Bristol, England, to ask why.

TELL US ABOUT YOUR FAMILY, RUPA.

Well, my dad is French and my mum is Indian. They are both chefs in different restaurants in town. They are very good at cooking.

1 ....

Sometimes it's my dad, sometimes it's my mum. Dad makes meals with a lot of courses. There's always a starter and a dessert – and there are usually four or five main courses, too! It's fantastic.

2 ....

She cooks traditional Indian food. We eat a lot of rice, and some lovely meat with sauces. Oh, and she makes great sweets.

3 ....

No, it's good for the same reason. People from all over the world live in England and they bring their food with them. There are a lot of different restaurants here.

4 ....

Yes! Here in Bristol is Za Za Bazaar. It's the biggest restaurant in the UK. They serve Mexican tacos, Japanese sushi, Italian pizza, American burgers – everything, really. Even typical British food.

5 ....

My favourite is fish and chips, of course. I'm English!

FACT! *In 1847 Joseph Fry made the world's first chocolate bar in Bristol.*

Reading A magazine interview

1 Look at the pictures. What do you think 'typical English food' is? Who are the people in the picture? Read the text and check your answers.

2 Put the questions in the correct place in the text.
1 And what about your mum?
2 Do you have a favourite restaurant?
3 What do you like to eat when you go there?
4 So who cooks in your house?
5 OK, so the food in your house is excellent. But what do you think about English food? Is it bad?

3 🔊 1.40 Read the interview with Rupa again and answer the questions.
1 Where are Rupa's parents from?
2 What do Rupa's parents do?
3 What's Rupa's favourite food?
4 What kind of food can you eat in Za Za Bazaar?

Explore international words

4 Find the words below in the text.

> sushi   pizza   taco   burger

Are they the same in your language? Can you think of any other international food words?

➔ Vocabulary bank • page 110

Your turn

5 Answer the questions for you. Then ask and answer with your partner.
1 What kind of food do you eat at home?
2 Who cooks in your house?
3 What kind of restaurants are there in your town?
4 What country does your favourite food come from?

> What kind of food do you eat at home?

> We eat Chinese and American food.

Speaking Ordering food

Real Talk: What do you usually have for lunch?

1 ▶ 4.3 Watch the teenagers in the video. How many of the teenagers talk about …
a) chicken   d) vegetables
b) pasta   e) fruit?
c) rice

2 What do *you* usually have for lunch? Ask and answer with your partner.

3 🔊 1.41 Listen to the conversation. What does Katy choose?

4 Complete the conversation with the useful language.

Useful language

I'd like …
Can I have …, please?
How much is that?
What can I get you?
Here you are.
What … would you like?
Anything else?

Waiter: Hi there. ¹…. you?
Katy: ²…. a sandwich, please?
Waiter: Of course. What filling ³…. ?
Katy: ⁴…. **spicy chicken**, please.
Waiter: Do you want it hot or cold?
Katy: **Hot**, please.
Waiter: Right. ⁵…. ?
Katy: Yes, please. A **cola**.
Waiter: OK. ⁶…. you ⁷…. .
Katy: ⁸…. ?
Waiter: **£3.35**, please.
Katy: Here you are.
Waiter: Thank you.

---

5 🔊 1.41 Listen again and check your answers.

6 Work with a partner. Practise the conversation in Exercise 4.

7 Change the words in bold in the conversation in Exercise 4. Use the information below. Practise the conversation.

• SANDWICH • CENTRAL

hot or cold sandwiches: **£2.25**
cheese and ham, spicy chicken, bacon, spicy Italian sausage, roast beef

drinks: **£1.10**
cola, lemonade, orange juice, coffee

Hi there, what can I get you?

Can I have a sandwich, please?

50

Writing A report

1 Look at the photo. What is Eva's celebration?

1 ....
I celebrate my birthday every year with a big birthday dinner at my house. My birthday is in June, so we usually have dinner in the garden. Before dinner, I always open my presents.

2 ....
First we have a starter. That's usually soup. After that, we have the main course. That's always fish, because fish is my favourite. Then we have ice cream and some lovely birthday cake.

3 ....
After that, we play games in the garden, and sometimes we go out to the cinema to watch a film. I love my birthday!

2 Read Eva's report. What do they eat on her birthday?

Useful language

Time connectors
Use time connectors *before*, *then* and *after that* when you describe the order of events.
  Before dinner, I always open my presents. After that, we have the main course. Then we have ice cream.

3 Find examples of time connectors in Eva's report.

4 Complete the text with the time connectors from the Useful language box.
¹ *Before* we go to the canteen for lunch, we put our bags in the classroom. ² .... we wait for hot or cold food. We choose what we want to eat and ³ .... we go and sit down at a table with our friends. ⁴ .... we eat our lunch and talk to our friends. ⁵ .... we put our plates away and go back to class.

5 Read Eva's report again. Put the paragraph headings in the right place.
- What we eat
- And after that
- When, where and who

Get Writing

PLAN

5 Make notes about a celebration meal. Include information about the things below.

| celebration | time | activities |
| people | food | place |

WRITE

6 Write your report. Use your notes and the language below.
When
It's in …
Where and who
We always … at …
We have dinner in … with …
What
First, we have … Then …
Other activities
Before dinner, … After that …, we …

CHECK

7 Can you say YES to these questions?
- Have you got information from Exercise 5 in your report?
- Have you got time connectors from the Useful language box?
- Are your spelling, grammar and vocabulary correct?

3–4 Review

Vocabulary

1 Match the activities with the places in school.

1. do outdoor sports
2. read books and do projects
3. meet with the whole school
4. have ICT classes
5. do experiments
6. have lunch
7. do indoor sports

a) canteen
b) science lab
c) sports hall
d) main hall
e) IT room
f) library
g) playing field

2 Write the school subjects in order from your favourite to your least favourite.

1. Science
2. Music
3. English
4. Maths
5. History
6. PE
7. Geography
8. French
9. ICT

3 Complete the food words.

dairy
1 c _hee_ s e   2 b _ _ _ _ r   3 m _ l _

fruit
4 _ ppl _   5 b _ n _ _ a

vegetables
6 b _ _ ns   7 c _ _ _ _ t

meat and fish
8 _ h _ _ k _ n   9 _ _ sh   10 b _ _ g _ r

other
11 b _ _ _ d   12 _ gg   13 _ _ zz _
14 p _ st _   15 r _ c _   16 t _ c _
17 s _ sh _

4 Which of the words in Exercise 3 are the same in your language?

5 Complete the sentences with the words in the box.

> breakfast   dessert   dinner   lunch
> main course   starter

1. The meal you have in the middle of the day is called .... .
2. My favourite .... is ice cream with bananas.
3. .... is the first meal of the day.
4. The big meal that people usually have in the evening is called .... .
5. Before the ...., we often have a .... .

6 Complete the crossword with nouns, verbs and adjectives.

Across
3. The opposite of *brilliant*.
5. You learn to be a teacher at a teacher .... college.
6. The opposite of *slow*.
7. An adjective meaning *very good*.

Down
1. What you do at school.
2. The verb of *practice*.
4. The opposite of *interesting*.

7 Match the sentences.

1. I always have
2. After dinner, I like to have a
3. I don't have a
4. 12 o'clock is very early

a) walk on the beach.
b) to have lunch.
c) fun when I meet my friends in the park.
d) problem with these Maths exercises – they're easy!

Language focus

1 Write sentences with the correct form of can.
1 *Can he ride a bike?*

1 he / ride a bike (?)
2 Maria / dance (✓)
3 we / go home (?)
4 Victor / play the guitar (✗)
5 you / swim (?)
6 they / do kung fu (✓)

2 Complete the text with the correct object pronouns.

Zara's my best friend. I like ¹ *her* and she likes ² .... ! We're in the same class. Our teacher is Mr Stevens. I don't like ³ .... because he gives ⁴ .... all lots of homework! Zara loves Art, but I hate ⁵ .... . Our friends like football and we often play with ⁶ .... after school.

3 Complete the sentences with the -ing form of the verbs in the box.

listen eat ~~do~~ play read ride

1 I don't like *doing* my homework after school.
2 I love .... games on my computer.
3 I hate .... in the school canteen.
4 I like .... Manga comics.
5 I love .... to music.
6 I don't mind .... my bike to school every day.

4 Which food and drink words on page 52 Exercise 3 are countable? Which are uncountable?
cheese: uncountable

5 Complete the sentences with a, an, some or any.
1 I sometimes have *a* banana for breakfast.
2 There's .... cheese in the fridge.
3 We don't eat .... meat, only vegetables.
4 Pete eats .... apple every day.
5 We haven't got .... salt. Can you go to the shops?
6 Can I have .... biscuits with my tea?
7 Are there .... tomatoes for a salad?
8 I always have .... biscuit with my tea.

6 Make questions or sentences with there is/there are. Use some or any.
1 *There's some milk.*

1 .... milk (✓)
2 .... cheese (✗)
3 .... eggs (?)
4 .... apples (✓)
5 .... chips (✗)
6 .... pasta (?)

7 Choose the correct options.
1 How **much / many** meat is there?
2 I haven't got **much / many** biscuits.
3 There are **a lot of / much** eggs. Let's make a tortilla.
4 There isn't **much / many** milk in the fridge.
5 How **much / many** potatoes do we need?
6 I've got **a lot of / many** bread. Do you want some?

Language builder

8 Complete the text with the correct word below.
Michelle doesn't eat ¹ .... fruit. She never has ² .... apple or ³ .... banana at lunch, but she loves ⁴ .... vegetables. There ⁵ .... always a lot of snacks in her lunch box, too. Tina has lunch at the same time as Michelle, so they ⁶ .... sit together. Tina usually has a cheese sandwich and a yoghurt. There ⁷ .... usually ⁸ .... fruit in her lunch box too. She doesn't eat ⁹ .... snacks. How ¹⁰ .... fruit do you eat every day? Do you eat ¹¹ .... vegetables?

1 a) much b) many
2 a) a   b) an
3 a) a   b) an
4 a) eat   b) eating
5 a) is   b) are
6 a) can   b) can't
7 a) is   b) are
8 a) any   b) some
9 a) much b) any
10 a) much b) many
11 a) a lot of b) much

Speaking

9 Choose the correct options.

Waiter: Hi. What ¹ **can I / do I** get you?
Mary: Yes, of course. I ² **'m like / 'd like** a salad sandwich, please and a glass of coke.
Waiter: OK.
Tom: And ³ **I'd like / I like** the spicy chicken, please.
Waiter: Right, ⁴ **anything / something** else?
Tom: Yes, please. A cup of coffee, please.
Mary: ⁵ **How many / How much** is that?
Waiter: £4 each, please.
Mary: Here ⁶ **you are / are you**. This is my £4.
Tom: Er, Mary, can I borrow some money please?
Mary: Sorry, Tom. I'm afraid you ⁷ **can't / don't**.
Tom: ⁸ **Why not / What not**?
Mary: Because I've only got £4!

5 Animal world

Discovery EDUCATION

In this unit …

- Shark attack! **p57**
- Animals in the city **p60** 
- Going to museums **p62** 
- CLIL Chameleons **p119** 

Vocabulary
- Animals
- Action verbs
- Adverbs of movement
- The suffix *er*

Language focus
- Present continuous
- Present simple vs Present continuous

Unit aims
I can …
- talk about animals.
- read and understand an animal quiz.
- make statements and ask and answer questions in the present continuous.
- understand a conversation about zoos.
- use the present simple or the present continuous correctly.
- ask for information in a shop.
- write a short description of an animal.

BE CURIOUS

What can you see in the photo?
Start thinking
- Where do polar bears live?
- What other animals live there?
- What other animals can swim?
- What animals can't swim?

Vocabulary Animals

1 🔊 **2.01** What is unusual about these animals? Label each picture with two animal names. Use the words in the box. Then listen, check and repeat.

> a bird   a cat   a cow   a dog   an elephant   a fish   a frog   a giraffe   a gorilla
> a horse (x2)   a monkey   a polar bear   a shark   a sheep   a spider   a tiger   a zebra

1 *a polar bear* and *a tiger*    2 …. and  ….   3 …. and ….

4 …. and 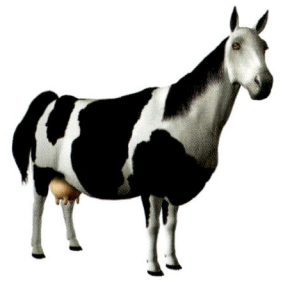 ….   5 …. and  ….   6 …. and ….

7 …. and  ….   8 …. and  ….   9 …. and ….

2 Copy and complete the table. Work with a partner. Put the animals in the correct columns. Some animals will go in more than one column.

Pets	Farm animals	Wild animals
birds		*birds*

Water animals	Land animals

➡ **Vocabulary bank** • page 111

👁 **Get it right!**

The plural forms of *fish* and *sheep* are irregular.
My sister's got two yellow fish.
There are 20 white sheep on the farm.
~~fishes~~ ✗   ~~sheeps~~ ✗

Your turn

3 Create an animal like the ones in Exercise 1. Draw a picture of it and describe it to a partner.

> My animal is part frog and part bird. It's small. It's green and red.

4 Listen to your partner's description. Draw his/her animal. Describe the animal to the class.

What are the animals doing?
ANIMAL ACTIONS QUIZ

Animals do different things for different reasons. Sometimes the reasons aren't what you think they are! How much do you know about animals' actions? Do this quiz and find out!

1 Why is this elephant moving its ears?
a It's tired.
b It's hot.
c It's afraid.

2 What's this horse doing?
a It's smiling.
b It's laughing.
c It's smelling something.

3 What are these giraffes doing?
a They're fighting.
b They're dancing.
c They're playing.

4 What's this frog doing?
a It's drinking.
b It's singing.
c It's eating.

5 What are these monkeys doing?
a They're playing.
b They're fighting.
c They're cleaning each other.

CLUES

Elephants move their ears backwards and forwards when they are hot and they want to stay cool.

Horses open their mouths and curl their lips when they want to smell something.

Frogs have a 'vocal sac' under their chins. Male frogs produce sounds from this sac and 'sing' to female frogs.

Giraffes use their long necks and their heads during fights over territory.

Monkeys often take insects and dirt out of each other's fur.

FACT! *Frogs live on every continent in the world except Antarctica.*

Reading A quiz

1 Look at the photos in the quiz. What animals can you see?

2 🔊 2.02 Read the quiz and answer the questions. Use the clues to help you.

3 🔊 2.03 Listen and check your answers to the quiz.

Explore adverbs of movement

4 Read the quiz again and underline the two adverbs of movement.

5 Complete the sentences with the adverbs from the text and in the box below.

> up   left   round (x2)   right   down

1 Elephants move their ears .... and .... to keep cool.
2 Look .... and .... before you cross the road.
3 Horses move their heads .... and .... when they're bored.
4 Dogs run .... and .... when they play.

➡ Vocabulary bank • page 111

Your turn

6 Work with a partner. Ask and answer the questions.
1 What information in the quiz is new to you?
2 What other animal actions do you know?

Language focus 1 Present continuous

1 Complete the examples from the text on page 56.

I	He / She / It	We / You / They
+	I **am watching** the animals.	The frog **is**	The monkeys **are** ....
–	I**'m not eating**.	The frog **isn't eating**.	The monkeys **aren't fighting**.
?	**Am** I **looking** at the mother elephant? Yes, I **am**. / No, I**'m** not.	Why .... the elephant .... its ears? **Is** the horse **smiling**? Yes, it **is**. / No, it **isn't**.	What .... the monkeys ....? **Are** the monkeys **fighting**? Yes, they **are**. / No, they **aren't**.

➡ Grammar reference • page 103

2 🔊 **2.04** Complete the text with the correct form of the present continuous. Use the verbs in brackets.

Hello, friends! Welcome to Animal World! Where am I? I'm in Vancouver, Canada! And, no, I ¹ *'m not talking* (not talk) to you from a swamp! Today, I ² .... (visit) the Vancouver Aquarium with my sister. Right now, we ³ .... (listen) to a guide. She ⁴ .... (talk) to some students about crocodiles. Oh, now the crocodiles ⁵ .... (get) very excited! It's lunchtime and our guide ⁶ .... (give) them some fish. She ⁷ .... (not go) very close to them, of course! The crocodiles are really hungry – they ⁸ .... (not share)! They ⁹ .... (show) their big teeth, and they ¹⁰ .... (eat) the fish very quickly!

3 💬 Write questions and answers with the present continuous form of the verbs. Then practise with a partner.

1 where / you / go — go / to the zoo
   Where are you going? *I'm going to the zoo.*
2 what / the sharks / do — eat / fish
3 Jen / feed / the horses — no
4 the cats / sleep — yes
5 what / the bird / doing — smell / a flower
6 you / walk / your dog — no

Your turn

4 Write three questions about what's happening in your class at the moment.
What is ... doing?
Is Maria ...ing?

5 Ask and answer the questions with your partner.

> What's the teacher doing?

> She's writing on the board.

Say it right!

a 🔊 **2.05** Listen and compare the different *g* sounds at the beginnings and ends of the words.
We're listenin**g** to a **g**uide.
The crocodiles are **g**ettin**g** very excited.

b 🔊 **2.06** Listen and repeat the sentences from Exercise 2. Pay close attention to the *-ing* sound.

Find out about sharks.
- How many different kinds of sharks can you see in the film?
- Where does the Greenland shark live?

Discovery EDUCATION
5.1 Shark attack

Listening A conversation

1 Do you go to the zoo? What animals do you see? What are your favourite zoo animals?

2 🔊 2.07 Listen to people talking at a zoo. What animals are they looking at? Write the number of the conversation next to the animals. Which of the animals *don't* they talk about?

elephants   birds   polar bears
monkeys   tigers   zebras

3 🔊 2.07 Listen again. Are the sentences true (*T*) or false (*F*)? Correct the false ones.
  1 It's OK to feed the birds. *F It isn't OK to feed the birds.*
  2 The monkeys are eating fruit. ....
  3 A big monkey is cleaning its mother. ....
  4 Elephants move their ears when they're cold. ....
  5 The father elephants live with their babies. ....
  6 The kids think the tiger is angry. ....

Vocabulary Action verbs

4 🔊 2.08 Match the action verbs to the pictures. Listen, check and repeat.

fight   fly   ~~hide~~   hunt   jump   swim   swing

5 🔊 2.09 Complete the sentences with the correct form of the verbs in Exercise 4. Listen, check and repeat.
  1 The snake is *hiding*.
  2 The turtle is ....
  3 The lion is ....
  4 The monkeys are ....
  5 The kangaroo is ....
  6 The parrots are ....
  7 The bears are ....

➔ **Vocabulary bank** • page 111

Your turn

6 Work with a partner. Ask and answer questions about what animals do.

> Do frogs fly? No, they don't.

Language focus 2 Present simple vs present continuous

1 Complete the examples from the listening on page 58.

Present simple for facts, habits and routines	Present continuous for activities that are happening at the moment
She **loves** her baby. They usually **fly** to warm places in the winter. It **doesn't like** its cage. Where **do** the fathers …. ?	It**'s eating** a banana. They**'re flying** really fast. They …. swinging from the trees. **Are** you **feeding** animals at the moment?
Common time expressions	
always usually …. sometimes never in the summer/spring/…./autumn on Monday/Tuesday/Friday	at the moment now ….

➡ **Grammar reference** • page 103

2 Choose the correct words to complete the sentences.
1 **I never feed** / I'm never feeding the animals at the zoo.
2 That snake **hides** / **is hiding** behind a tree right now.
3 Kangaroos **usually live** / **are usually living** in groups.
4 **Do you look at** / **Are you looking at** the tigers now?
5 The guide **gives** / **is giving** a tour of the aquarium at the moment.
6 Bears **sleep** / **are sleeping** in the winter.

3 Complete the email with the present simple or present continuous of the verbs in brackets.

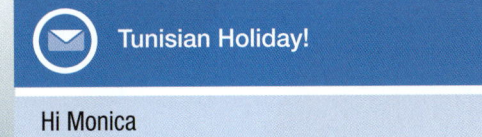

✉ Tunisian Holiday!   Monica ▶

Hi Monica
How are you? We ¹ **'re having** (have) a great time here in Tunisia. Look at this photo! My sister and I ² …. (ride) a camel! It's funny because my sister ³ …. (not like) animals – but you can see that she ⁴ …. (enjoy) the ride.
I ⁵ …. (write) this email on the computer in the hotel. It ⁶ …. (be) a small place, but we ⁷ …. (like) it. We always ⁸ …. (stay) here when we come to Tunisia. It ⁹ …. (have) a lovely swimming pool. Mum and Dad ¹⁰ …. (swim) in it right now.
I' ¹¹ …. (go) now, because my mum ¹² …. (call) me.
Write soon!
Love,
Miranda ▶

👁 Get it right!

We usually use these verbs in the present simple, not the present continuous.

> be   have (for possession)
> love   see   understand

I love animals. Not *I'm loving animals.*

Your turn

4 Student A: Draw a picture of an animal.

Student B: While Student A is drawing, ask questions about the animals.

> Are you drawing a cat?

> Yes.

> Is it climbing a tree?

5 What facts do you know about the animal? Tell your partner.

> Cats eat mice. They sleep during the day.

Discover Culture

1 Match the animals to the pictures 1–6. Which ones do you like? Which ones are you afraid of? Why? Why not?

> rat spider crocodile snake camel lion

2 Which of the animals do you find on the streets of India?

Find out about how animals and humans live and work together.

Discovery EDUCATION
5.2 Animals in the city

3 5.2 Watch the video and check your answers to Exercise 2. What other animals can you see in the video? Which of the animals live …
- on the streets? *horse*
- in the wild? *lion*

4 5.2 Watch the video again. Are the sentences about rats (R), snakes (S) or both (B)?
1. People often give food to them. *B*
2. They are welcome in people's houses.
3. People think they are very special.
4. People respect them.
5. They eat nuts and drink milk.
6. People know how to work with them.
7. People hold a festival with them.

5 Test your memory. Which of these scenes do you see in the video?
a) Cows sitting on the pavement.
b) A camel carrying a cart.
c) Rats drinking water.
d) A snake crawling into a pot.
e) An elephant with a blue and yellow painted face.

6 Choose the best summary of the video.
- Frightening animals in India
- Animals and Indian culture
- Living with dangerous animals

Your turn

7 Work with a partner. Which animals can you find on the streets of your city? Which animals can you find in the countryside near your city?

> In my town, there are birds and maybe rats at night!

8 Which animal from the video do you like best? Why?

HUSKIES
THE INUIT'S HELPER

UNIT 5

Husky dogs are more than just animals to some people. Huskies can help in a lot of different ways.

The native people of the Arctic are called the *Inuit*. They live in Alaska, Canada and Greenland. They live in very cold climates. The Inuit people use huskies because the dogs are strong and can live in very cold climates, too. They are also very good workers.

Today, a lot of Inuit people live a traditional lifestyle. They use animals for food, transport, and clothes. In the Arctic, there aren't many vegetables or fruit. In fact, in some places, there aren't any supermarkets. The basic diet of the Inuit people is meat and fish. The Inuit hunt seals, polar bears and reindeer, and their huskies help them. Inuit hunters travel with their dogs. They make sledges with animal bones and skin, and teams of huskies pull the sledges. These dogs can pull heavy sledges and go very fast.

Of all the animals in the Arctic, the husky is the Inuit's greatest helper!

Reading An article

FACT! *A team of huskies with a sledge can travel over 150 km in one day.*

1 Look at the title, map and pictures. Where do the dogs live? What is the weather like?

2 🔊 2.10 Read the article. How do huskies help the Inuit people? What do the Inuit use other animals for?

3 Read the article again and correct the sentences.
  1 The Inuit use reindeer to pull their sledges.
  2 They make sledges with wood.
  3 The Inuit eat a lot of fruit and vegetables.
  4 They hunt seals, sharks and reindeer.

5 Make more *-er* words. What do you call a person who …
  1 dances? a *dancer*   3 sings? a ….
  2 drives? a ….   4 teaches? a ….

→ **Vocabulary bank** • page 111

Your turn

6 Make a list of animals that people use for work in your country. What work do they do?

> The police sometimes use dogs to help them.

Explore the suffix *-er.*

4 Read the article again and underline all the words ending in *-er*. Are they
  a) verbs   b) nouns   c) adjectives ?

Take the *-er* off each word. Is the word a verb, a noun or an adjective?

Speaking Asking for and giving directions

Real Talk: Do you like going to museums?

1 5.3 Watch the teenagers in the video. How many people like …

museums	art galleries	history museums	science museums	aquariums	zoos

2 Do *you* like going to museums? Ask and answer with your partner.

3 2.11 Listen to the conversation. Where is the frog exhibit? Listen and check.

4 Complete the conversation with the useful language.

Useful language

It's on …   How do I get to … ?
Take …   Turn …

5 2.11 Listen again and check your answers.

6 Work with a partner. Practise the conversation in Exercise 4.

7 Work with a partner. Change the words in bold in the conversation in Exercise 4. Use the information below. Practise the conversation.

Stella: Excuse me. ¹…. **the frog exhibit**?
Guide: Oh, that's easy. Walk down this hall.
Stella: OK.
Guide: ²…. **left** at the end of the hall.
Stella: OK, go **straight down** the hall, and then **left**. Then what?
Guide: ³…. **the stairs up to the third floor**.
Stella: OK. Thanks. Is the **frog exhibit at the top of the stairs**?
Guide: Yes, it is. ⁴…. **the right**.
Stella: Great. Thank you.
Guide: You're welcome.

Bird Gallery — Stairs / Lifts — Insect Gallery (3rd floor)
Reptile Gallery — Stairs / Lifts — Dinosaur Gallery (2nd floor)
Cloakroom — Stairs / Lifts — Café (1st floor)
Toilets — Stairs — Shop (You are here, Ground Floor)

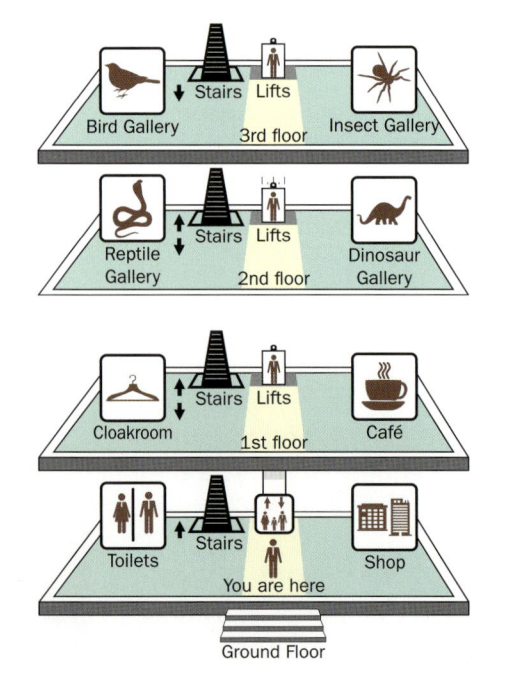

Writing A description of an animal

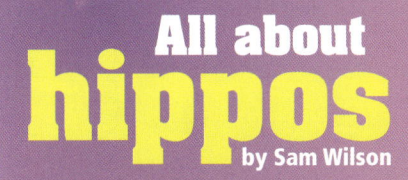

All about hippos
by Sam Wilson

Wild hippopotamuses live in central Africa. They're big and fat. They have small eyes, small ears and short legs. They also have very big teeth! Adult hippos are usually three to four metres long, and they can run very fast!

The hippo in the photo is sleeping in the water. Hippos often sleep in water during the day because the water is cool. Hippos usually come out of the water at night and eat. They only eat plants. They can eat up to 40 kg of grass in one night, and they can travel up to 10 km to find food. Hippos can be very dangerous. Every year they kill hundreds of people!

1 Look at the photo. Why is the hippo sleeping in the water? Read the text and check your answer.

2 Copy the table. Then write the information in the order it appears in the text.

> interesting facts about the animal   ~~where it lives~~
> what it eats   what it looks like   its daily activities

1	where it lives	Central Africa
2		
3		
4		
5		

3 Read the description again. What information does Sam include for each category in Exercise 2?

Useful language

Position of adjectives
Use adjectives …
- after *is* or *are*: They're **big** and **fat**.
- before a noun: They have **small** eyes.
- after *very*: Hippos can be **very** *dangerous*.

4 Find examples of adjectives in the description in Exercise 1.

5 Put the words in order to make sentences.
   1 *I've got a big cat.*
   1 cat / I've / big / a / got
   2 the tiger / animal / dangerous / is / a
   3 big / has / ears / the elephant / got
   4 are / very / gorillas / strong
   5 are / and orange / giraffes / brown

Get Writing

PLAN

6 Make a word web about an animal. Include information from Exercise 2. Find or draw a picture of your animal.

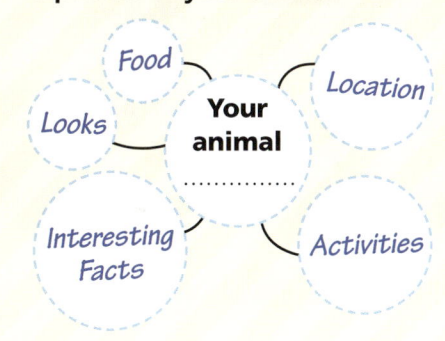

- Food
- Looks
- Location
- Your animal
- Interesting Facts
- Activities

WRITE

7 Write a description of your animal. Use your notes and the language below.

[My animals] live in …
They're …
They have …
They eat …
etc.

CHECK

8 Can you say YES to these questions?
- Have you got information from Exercise 6 in your description?
- Are the adjectives in the correct places?
- Are your spelling, grammar and vocabulary correct?

6 City life

Discovery EDUCATION

In this unit ...

- Rome: ancient and modern **p67**
- Crossing cities **p70**
- Activities with friends **p72**
- CLIL Big art **p120**

Vocabulary
- Places in a town
- Transport
- Extreme adjectives
- Collocations

Language focus
- Past simple of *be*
- *There was/were*
- Past simple regular and irregular affirmative/negative

Unit aims
I can ...
- talk about places in a town.
- read and understand an article about Pompeii.
- talk about the past.
- ask questions about routines and activities.
- understand a presentation about a town.
- talk about methods of transport.
- understand an article about transport in big cities.
- use sequencing devices.
- write a description of a place.

BE CURIOUS
What can you see in the photo?
Start thinking
- Do you like cities? Why/Why not?
- What is the biggest city in your country?
- What are the advantages and disadvantages of living in a city?

Vocabulary Places in a town 1

1 🔊 **2.12** Match the pictures with the places in the box. Then listen, check and repeat. Which place isn't in the photos?

> shopping centre   museum   cinema   sports stadium
> bowling alley   market   sports centre   skate park

2 🔊 **2.13** Listen to the sounds and match them with the places in the pictures.

Your turn

3 Copy and complete the table with information about you.

	Me	My partner
What's your favourite place in town?	*sports centre*	
How often do you go there?		
Who do you go with?		
What do you do there?		

4 Ask and answer the questions with a partner and complete the table with your partner's information.

➡ **Vocabulary bank • page 112**

POMPEII

In AD 79, Pompeii was a large town in Italy, with a population of about 20,000. On the evening of August 24th, there was a very big volcanic eruption. The eruption destroyed the town.

This is how Pompeii looks today. It's an open-air museum and it's very popular with tourists. The town is in ruins, but you can still see the remains of the ancient streets and houses. You can imagine life two thousand years ago! You can also see people preserved by the boiling volcanic ash with terrified expressions on their faces.

Before the eruption, Pompeii was a very busy town, and the people were rich. There were shops, squares, schools and markets. There was an enormous amphitheatre – a type of sports stadium. The amphitheatre was a very important place in the town. On special days it was full of people, gladiators and lions. It wasn't a very safe place to go!

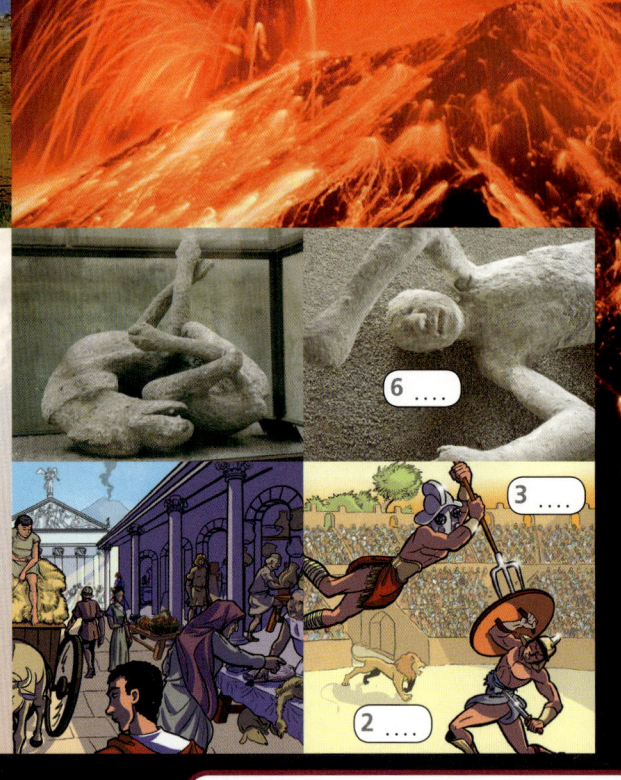

FACT! *About 2.5 million tourists visit Pompeii every year. It is often called The City of the Dead.*

Reading An information text

1 Look at the pictures. Where is Pompeii? Can you find these things in the pictures?

> ruins   gladiator   volcano   eruption   ash   amphitheatre

2 🔊 **2.14** Read the text. Check your ideas in Exercise 1.

3 Are the sentences true (*T*) or false (*F*)? Correct the false ones.
1 There is a large volcano near Pompeii.
2 There are a lot of museums in Pompeii.
3 You can still see a lot of the old town.
4 The amphitheatre is often full of lions and gladiators.

Explore extreme adjectives

4 Look at the text. Find words which mean:
a) very big
b) very old
c) very hot
d) very scared

5 Complete the sentences with the words above.
1 Ouch! I can't eat this soup – it's .... !
2 The new sports stadium is .... . It can hold 80,000 people.
3 There is an .... castle in my town.
4 I was .... when the lion escaped from its cage!

➔ **Vocabulary bank** • page 112

Your turn

6 Work with a partner. Ask and answer the questions.
1 What ancient ruins are there in your country?
2 How old are they?
3 How often do you go there?

Language focus 1 was/were, there was/were

1 Complete the examples from the text on page 66.

	Singular	Plural
+	Pompeii .... a very busy town. There .... an enormous amphitheatre.	The shops and markets **were** always busy. There .... shops and markets.
–	It .... a safe place to go. There **wasn't** a swimming pool.	The people .... rich. There **weren't** any shops.
?	**Was** the amphitheatre in the centre? Yes, it **was**. / No, it **wasn't**. **Was there** a swimming pool? Yes, **there was**. / No, **there wasn't**.	**Were** the people rich? Yes, they **were**. / No, they **weren't**. **Were there** any shops? Yes, **there were**. / No, **there weren't**.

➡ **Grammar reference** • page 104

2 Complete the sentences with *was(n't)* or *were(n't)*.
1. The amphitheatre *was* very popular in ancient Pompeii.
2. There .... shops and schools in Pompeii.
3. Christopher Columbus and Vasco da Gama .... famous explorers.
4. There .... any cars in ancient Pompeii. (not)
5. Neil Armstrong .... an American astronaut.
6. The population of Rome .... 2 million in AD 79. (not)

3 Rewrite the sentences with the information in brackets.
1. *Nelson Mandela wasn't Chinese. He was South African.*

1. Nelson Mandela was Chinese. (South African)
2. Tolstoy and Chekov were painters. (writers)
3. Mustafa Ataturk was from Poland. (Turkey)
4. Lasar Segall and Lygia Clark were singers. (artists)

4 💬 Work with a partner. Ask and answer questions about the people in Exercise 3.

> Was Nelson Mandela Chinese?

> No, he wasn't. He was South African.

👁 Get it right!
We use *any* with questions and negatives.
Were there any cinemas in Pompeii?
There weren't **any** cinemas in Pompeii.

5 Write sentences about Pompeii in AD 79. Use *there was(n't)/were(n't)* and the words in the box.

> sports stadium ✗   an amphitheatre ✓   houses ✓
> an open-air museum ✗   markets ✓   car parks ✗
> schools ✓   cinemas ✗

There wasn't a sports stadium in Pompeii in AD 79.

Your turn

6 Complete the questions and answer them.
1. Who *was* the first person in class today?
2. Which day of the week .... your last birthday on?
3. Who .... your best friends at primary school?
4. Where .... you and your friends on Saturday?
5. Where .... you at 11 o'clock last night?

7 Ask and answer with your partner.

Find out about the historic city of Rome.
- How many people visit Rome every year?
- What happened in the Colosseum?
- How many people went to the events at the Colosseum?

Discovery EDUCATION

6.1 Rome: ancient and modern

UNIT 6

Vocabulary Places in a town 2

1 🔊 **2.15** Match the words in the box with the places (1–7) on the map. Then listen, check and repeat.

1 *ferry port*

> bus stop   car park   bus station   ~~ferry port~~
> station   tram stop   market

2 How is this town different from yours?
In my town there isn't a ferry port.

3 Write sentences about the town. Use the prepositions in the box.

> opposite   behind   next to   in front of

The bus stop is opposite the park.

Listening A report

4 🔊 **2.16** Listen to Jamie talking about his class trip to this town. Write the places in the order that he speaks about them.

1 *sports stadium*

> bowling alley   ~~sports stadium~~   park   station
> shopping centre   ferry port   school   museum

5 🔊 **2.16** Listen again. Answer the questions with short answers.

1 *Yes, it was.*

1 Was the town a fishing village 100 years ago?
2 Was there a football match on the day of the trip?
3 Were there any interesting things in the museum?
4 Were there any children at the school?
5 Was the train home at 6 o'clock?

Your turn

6 Draw a plan of your town or city.

7 Work with a partner. Ask and answer questions about your partner's plan. Use the prepositions from Exercise 3.

> Where is the school?   It's next to the museum.

Vocabulary bank • page 112

Language focus 2 Past simple: regular and irregular verbs

1 Complete the examples from the listening on page 68.

I / You / He / She / It / We / They	
Regular verbs	Irregular verbs
+ We **arrived** at the station at 10 o'clock. We .... two games.	We **went** to the museum first. We .... lunch in the park.
– We .... **visit** the sports centre. We .... football.	We **didn't go** there. I .... any money.

➔ **Grammar reference • page 104**

2 🔊 **2.17** Complete the sentences with the past simple of the verbs in the box. Then listen and check.

> go   take   ~~play~~   eat   visit   walk

1 *played*
1 We .... football for three hours yesterday.
2 I .... hundreds of photos on the school trip.
3 We .... lots of cake at the party.
4 I .... my grandmother last weekend.
5 We .... five kilometres on the school trip yesterday!
6 We .... on a school trip to the zoo – it was great!

➔ **Irregular verbs list • page 127**

3 Change the sentences in Exercise 2 into negatives.

1 *We didn't play football for three hours yesterday.*

Say it right!

🔊 **2.18** Listen and put the words with the correct sound. Then listen, check and repeat.

/t/	/d/	/ɪd/
liked		

Your turn

4 Write true sentences for you about last weekend. Use the ideas below.

- go to the cinema
- sleep for ten hours on Saturday night
- go to a shopping centre
- play a musical instrument
- eat a salad

Last weekend I went to the cinema.

ago

We use *ago* to say how far back in the past something happened.

5 Complete the example from the listening on page 68.

It was a small fishing village 100 years .... .

➔ **Grammar reference • page 104**

6 Write sentences with *ago*.

1 *The train arrived 5 minutes ago.*

1 The train / arrive / 5 minutes
2 Leonardo / paint / the *Mona Lisa* / about 500 years
3 I / finish / my project / a week
4 We / leave / primary school / 2 years

Your turn

7 Write true sentences for you. Use *ago*.

- this lesson / start
- I / eat / breakfast
- I / get / out of bed
- I / learn / to walk
- my parents / meet

8 Work with a partner. Compare your sentences.

> My parents met seventeen years ago.

> Oh, my parents met twenty years ago!

Discover Culture

1 Match the pictures 1–6 with the words.

> underground   bullet train   aeroplane
> traffic jam   zebra crossing   tuk-tuk/rickshaw

2 Match the transport words in Exercise 1 with the cities.

> Mumbai (India)   Tokyo (Japan)   Beijing (China)

Find out about methods of transport around the world.

6.2 Crossing cities

3 6.2 Watch the video about transport in the three cities and check your answers to Exercise 2.

4 6.2 Watch the video again and put these fast-moving images in order.
a) a taxi ride at night
b) an aerial view of a city and clouds
c) a fast train with a mountain in the background
d) a lot of traffic crossing a bridge
e) a passenger jet at an airport
f) an aerial view of a city at night with traffic

5 6.2 Complete the sentences with the correct numbers. Then watch again and check your answers.
1 Mumbai and Beijing have a population of more than …. million.
2 Tokyo's bullet train travels at …. kilometres per hour.
3 Every day, …. new cars travel the streets of Beijing.
4 Tokyo's population is about …. million.
5 …. million people travel every day by train in Mumbai.

6 Match the sentences to the three different cities.

> Beijing   Mumbai   Tokyo

1 You can find so many types of transport there, some are very colourful!
2 A lot of people travel there for work by plane, but a lot of people walk too!
3 There are lots of cars. Every day there is more traffic on the streets!

Your turn

7 Work with a partner. Ask and answer the questions.
1 Which is your favourite form of transport? Why?
2 Which is the best for travelling round a city? Why?
3 Which do you use most often?

Reading A blog

1 Look at the map and the pictures. How do people travel to work and to school in this city? Is it easy? Read David's blog and check your answers.

2 Look at the map of Hong Kong. Read the text again and draw David's route to school in the mornings.

3 🔊 **2.19** Read the text again. Choose the correct answers.
   1 Yesterday, David travelled **on foot / on the underground** first.
   2 David's favourite method of transport is **the ferry / the tram**.
   3 David **took / didn't take** the bus up to the Mid-Levels yesterday.
   4 David prefers the escalator because it's **quick / fun**.

Explore collocations

4 Look at the highlighted words in the text. Complete the paragraph below with the correct words.

When I was at primary school, I always went to school ¹.... foot. Now that I am at secondary school, I usually travel to school ².... bus because it's a long way away. Some of my friends ³.... the tram to school and others come by bike. I want a bike for my birthday, because I don't like going ⁴.... bus every morning.

➡ **Vocabulary bank** • page 112

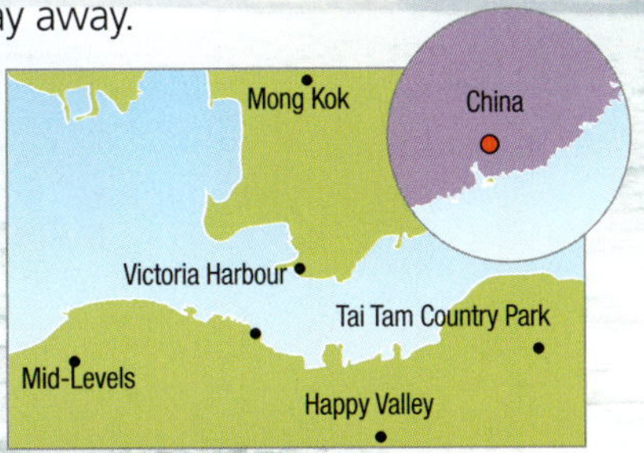

Your turn

5 Copy and complete the chart about journeys to school so it's true for you.

David Wong	You	Your partner
foot, underground, ferry, tram, escalator		
45 minutes		

6 Tell your partner how you travelled to school yesterday. Write your partner's answers in the chart.

> I went to school by bus. It took …

GETTING AROUND IN Hong Kong

Today we're looking at unusual journeys to school. Twelve-year-old David Wong tells us about his journey to school in Hong Kong.

I live in Mong Kok in Kowloon, Hong Kong. A lot of people live in Mong Kok and everybody uses public transport. In the rush hour, it's very busy. My school's a long way away, on the other side of the city. I travel on all the city's public transport to get to school. I don't take any money because I've got an Octopus Card. It's called the Octopus Card because an octopus has eight legs and eight is a lucky number in China.

Yesterday was a normal school day. I went **on foot** from my flat to the underground station in Mong Kok. Then I **took the ferry** across Victoria Harbour. I arrived on the island side, and I **took the tram**. I like travelling **by tram** best because you get a great view from the top! Finally, I went **on foot** up the escalator to my school in the Mid-Levels. Some students go **by bus**, but the escalator is more fun. The whole journey was only 45 minutes!

FACT! People in Hong Kong make 12 million journeys on public transport every day.

Speaking Sequencing

Real Talk: Where do you usually go with your friends?

1 🎬 **6.5** Watch the teenagers in the video. How many of the teenagers …
a) go to the shopping centre or mall?
b) eat or drink something?
c) go to their friends' houses?
d) go to the park?

2 💬 Where do *you* usually go with your friends? Ask and answer with a partner.

3 🔊 **2.20** Listen to the conversation. What did Charlie and David do at the weekend?

4 Complete the conversation with the useful language.

> **Useful language**
>
> After that   So you …   First   Really?   Then

5 🔊 **2.20** Listen again and check your answers.

6 💬 Work with a partner. Practise the conversation in Exercise 4.

7 💬 Work with a partner. Change the helicopter ride in Exercise 4 to another exciting activity and practise the conversation. Use the ideas below or your own ideas.

Charlie: What did you do at the weekend?
David: Oh, it was so cool!
Charlie: ¹…. ?
David: Yes. I went on a helicopter!
Charlie: Wow!
David: It was a big surprise.
Charlie: ²…. didn't know about it before?
David: No. ³…. we all got in the car at 8 o'clock. ⁴…., an hour later, we arrived at the airport.
Charlie: Cool.
David: And there was the helicopter! We flew over our house. It was amazing.
Charlie: What did you do then?
David: ⁵…. Dad drove home. What did *you* do at the weekend?
Charlie: Homework!

What did you do at the weekend?

Oh, it was so cool!

UNIT 6

✏️ Writing A description of a place

1 Look at the photos. Where do you think this town is?

2 Read Kirstie's email to Nicole. Check your answers to Exercise 1. What can you do in Kirstie's town?

▶ Nicole

Hi Nicole
Here's some info about my town for your visit next term.

1 ....
Tavistock is a small town with a population of about 11,000. It's in a place in England called Devon.

2 ....
It has an interesting history. Sir Francis Drake was from Tavistock. He was a famous English explorer in the 16th century. He was also the second person to sail all the way around the world.

3 ....
There are a lot of historical buildings in Tavistock and a museum, too. In May, there's a music and arts festival, so we can go to some free concerts. We can also visit Dartmoor National Park! It's beautiful. There are lots of shops, parks and sports facilities, too.
See you in May!
Kirstie

▶ Kirstie

---

3 Put the paragraph headings in the correct place in Kirstie's email.
- Things to do and places to visit
- History and interesting facts
- Size and location

Useful language

Adding information
Use *also* and *too* to add more information. They have the same meaning, but are in different positions in the sentence.
- *also* goes after the verb *be* and before other main verbs
  We can *also* visit Dartmoor National Park.
- *too* goes at the end of a sentence
  There are lots of shops, parks and sports facilities, *too*.

4 Find more examples of *also* and *too* in the text in Exercise 2.

5 Rewrite the sentences using *also* or *too*.
  1 *There's also an amusement park to visit.*
  1 There's an amusement park to visit, too.
  2 We can also go to the mountains.
  3 We also have a carnival in August.
  4 Lots of people visit the beautiful beaches, too.
  5 They make traditional products, too.

✏️ Get Writing

PLAN

6 Make notes about your town. Include information from Exercise 3.

WRITE

7 Write your email. Use your notes from Exercise 6, and the language below.

Size and location
It's a big / small / town / city in …
History / interesting facts
It's famous for …
We've got …
Things to do / places to visit
There is / are … also … too

CHECK

8 Can you say YES to these questions?
- Have you got information from Exercise 6 in your description?
- Are *also* and *too* in the correct position?
- Did you use past simple verbs?
- Are your spelling, grammar and vocabulary correct?

5-6 Review

Vocabulary

1 Write sentences about the pictures. Use an animal from box *a* and a verb from box *b*.

a) birds   cat   frog   polar bears   rat   ~~tiger~~

b) escaping   fighting   flying   hiding   ~~hunting~~   jumping

1   *The tiger is hunting.*

2 Complete the sentences with the words in the box.

up and down   round and round
left and right   backwards and forwards

1   The girl's name HANNAH reads the same ….
2   The wheels on a bike go ….
3   Running …. the stairs is hard work.
4   Turn your head slowly …. so that you can see all around you.

3 How many *-er* words can you remember from page 61? Write a sentence for each one.
A hunter hunts.

4 Match the activities with the places.

1   *d*

1   watch a match   a) museum
2   see a film   b) sports centre
3   buy some jeans   c) skate park
4   play basketball   d) sports stadium
5   learn about history   e) the cinema
6   wear a helmet!   f) shopping centre
7   buy some fresh vegetables   g) bowling alley
8   go bowling   h) market

5 Write the name of each type of transport. Then match them with the correct places.

park   port   ~~stand~~   station   stop (x2)

1   *bike / bike stand*

6 Match the adjectives with the definitions.

1   enormous   a) very scared
2   ancient   b) very old
3   terrified   c) very hot
4   boiling   d) very big

7 Complete the text with the words below.

on (x2)   by (x2)   took (x2)

It took me a long time to get to my grandparents' house. First I went ¹…. foot from my house to the bus stop. Then I ²…. the bus to the station. The journey ³…. train took two hours. I had lunch ⁴…. the train, and then I ⁵…. a taxi to my grandparents' village. I stayed with them for a week, and while I was there I went everywhere ⁶…. bike. I'm glad I like travelling!

74

Language focus

1 Write sentences and questions with the present continuous. Complete the short answers.

I'm learning English now.

1. I / learn English / now
2. They / not study / at the moment
3. She / not sleep / now
4. A: What / they / eat?
   B: They / eat / sandwiches.
5. A: you / do / your homework?
   B: Yes, …. .
6. A: he / phone / his friend?
   B: No, …. .

2 Complete the sentences and questions with the present simple or present continuous. Use the verbs in brackets.

1. Mike *listens* to music every day. (listen)
2. Anna …. a book now. (read)
3. We …. dinner at the moment. (not eat)
4. I …. TV on weekdays. (not watch)
5. What …. they …. now? (do)
6. What time …. he usually …. to bed? (go)
7. …. you …. on the computer now? (play)
8. …. they usually …. up at 6 pm? (get)

3 Complete the sentences with *was(n't)* or *were(n't)*.

1. A: *Was* Sarah at school yesterday?
   B: Yes, she …. .
2. A: …. you at home last weekend?
   B: No, we …. .
3. A: Where …. Mike last week?
   B: He …. on holiday.
4. A: The bus …. late this morning.
   B: …. you late for school?
5. A: …. there a lot of homework yesterday?
   B: No, there …. .
6. A: There …. a lot of children at the shopping centre.
   B: It's the summer holidays.
7. A: There …. a bottle of lemonade in the fridge yesterday.
   B: I drank it, sorry!
8. A: …. there any football matches last weekend?
   B: No, there …. .

4 Write true sentences about you with the verbs in brackets and *ago*.

1. *I went on holiday six months ago.*

1. (go on) holiday
2. (listen) to music
3. (not go) shopping
4. (tidy) my bedroom
5. (travel) by bus
6. (eat) Italian food
7. (not fly) in an aeroplane
8. (not forget) my homework

Language builder

5 Choose the correct words to complete the conversation.

Karen:	Hi, Judy. What ¹ **do you do / are you doing**?
Judy:	² **I watch / I'm watching** TV. There's a film about polar bears on. Two baby polar bears ³ **try / are trying** to walk but they ⁴ **aren't doing / don't do** very well. They're so cute.
Karen:	I know! There ⁵ **was / were** a film about the Arctic on TV last week, too. I ⁶ **see / saw** lots of baby polar bears! So sweet!
Judy:	Oh, I ⁷ **don't / didn't** watch that one.
Karen:	Pity. ⁸ **Do you usually watch / Are you usually watching** TV in the afternoon, Judy?
Judy:	No, ⁹ **I don't / I'm not**. I usually ¹⁰ **am going / go** to the pool on Saturdays, but today I can't. My parents ¹¹ **go / went** to London this morning, so I ¹² **look / 'm looking** after my little sister right now.

Speaking

6 Complete the conversation with the words in the box.

| You're welcome | take | After that |
| How do I get to | turn | it's on | First |

Susan:	Excuse me. ¹ …. the cinema?
Police officer:	That's easy. ² …. , walk to the end of this street.
Susan:	OK.
Police officer:	Then ³ …. left and walk about 200 metres.
Susan:	Then what?
Police officer:	⁴ …. go into the shopping centre and ⁵ …. the stairs.
Susan:	Is the cinema at the top of the stairs?
Police officer:	Yes, ⁶ …. the left.
Susan:	Thanks very much.
Police officer:	⁷ …. .

7 Sport

Discovery EDUCATION

In this unit …

- The Palio **p79** 
- The bowler **p82** 
- Talking about the weekend **p84** 
- CLIL Extreme fishing **p121**

Vocabulary
- Sports and activities
- Clothes
- Adverbs
- Irregular plurals

Language focus
- Past simple *Yes/No* questions
- Past simple *Wh-* questions

Unit aims
I can …
- talk about sports and activities.
- read and understand about sumo wrestling.
- ask and answer *yes/no* questions in the past.
- understand a conversation about a sports event.
- talk about clothes.
- ask and answer *Wh-* questions in the past.
- write a short biography.

BE CURIOUS

What can you see in the photo?
Start thinking
- What is the person in the picture doing?
- Do you know anyone who does this sport?
- What other exciting sports do you know?

Vocabulary Sports and activities

1 🔊 2.21 Label the pictures with the sports words in the box. Then listen, check and repeat.

> do judo   go bowling   go cycling   go skateboarding   go skiing   go snowboarding
> go surfing   go windsurfing   play baseball   ~~play basketball~~   play volleyball

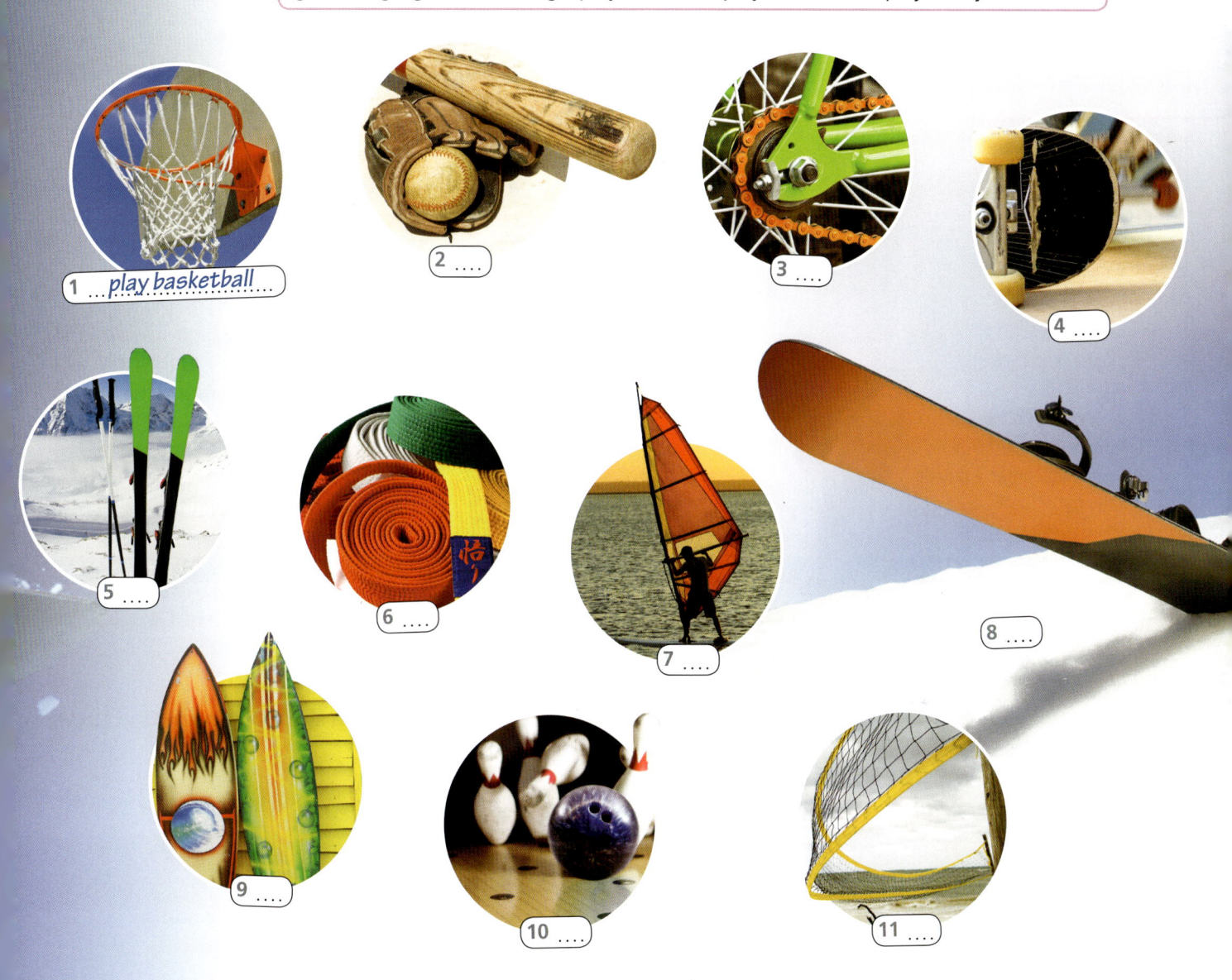

1 ...play basketball...
2 ....
3 ....
4 ....
5 ....
6 ....
7 ....
8 ....
9 ....
10 ....
11 ....

2 Look again at the sports in Exercise 1. Which ones …
1 are water sports?
2 are sports with a ball?
3 need something with wheels?
4 need a board?
5 are team sports?
6 are individual sports?

Get it right!

Let's **play** football / basketball / tennis.
Let's **do** judo / karate / yoga.
~~Let's play yoga.~~ ✗
~~I play skiing.~~ ✗

Your turn

3 Work with a partner. Ask and answer the questions.
1 What sports do you do?
2 Where do you do them?
3 When do you do them?
4 Who do you do them with?

> What sports do you do?

> I play basketball. I also ski.

➡ **Vocabulary bank • page 113**   77

SPORTS EVENTS

SUMO GIANTS

What do you know about sumo wrestling? Here are some FAQs about sumo wrestling (Frequently Asked Questions – or questions people often ask).

SUMO: FAQs

1. Did the sport start in China?
2. Is sumo an old or a new sport?
3. How many professional wrestlers are there in Japan?
4. Can women wrestle?
5. Do children do sumo wrestling?
6. How much do the wrestlers weigh?
7. How many times a day do they eat?
8. What do they eat?

Answers

a. It's a very old sport. It probably started 2000 years ago, but it first became a spectator sport in the 17th century.
b. They usually eat *chankonabe*, a traditional dish with chicken, fish, beef, tofu and a lot of vegetables. They also eat a lot of rice.
c. No, they can't. Traditionally, only men can be professional sumo wrestlers.
d. Yes, they do. You can be a professional wrestler from the age of fifteen. But sumo isn't very popular with children in Japan today. Japanese children generally prefer football, judo, and baseball.
e. They usually weigh between 120 and 150 kilos. They are very big men!
f. They typically eat twice a day. Sumo wrestlers don't eat breakfast and they often sleep after lunch.
g. No, sumo didn't start in China. It comes from very old Japanese traditions.
h. There are about 700. Not all of the wrestlers are from Japan. Surprisingly, there are wrestlers from Hawaii, Mongolia, Bulgaria, Russia, and other countries.

FACT! A typical 13-year-old needs about 2,000–2,500 calories a day. A sumo wrestler eats about 20,000 calories a day!

Reading FAQs about sumo wrestlers

1. 🔊 2.22 Work with a partner. Read the FAQs about sumo wrestling. Do you know any of the answers?

2. 🔊 2.23 Match the questions with the answers. Then listen and check.

3. Read the questions and answers again. Are the sentences true (*T*) or false (*F*)? Correct the false ones.
   1. *F – they eat two meals a day.*
   1. Sumo wrestlers eat three meals a day.
   2. There aren't any professional women sumo wrestlers.
   3. Japanese children today love sumo wrestling.
   4. Sumo wrestlers don't sleep during the day.
   5. Sumo wrestling isn't from China.
   6. All sumo wrestlers are from Japan.

Explore adverbs

4. Read the answers in the FAQ again. Find these adverbs.

   > usually   surprisingly   typically   generally   traditionally

5. Three of these adverbs have the same meaning. What are they?
   usually, …. , ….

➔ Vocabulary bank • page 113

Your turn

6. Make notes about your sports habits. Tell your partner about your sports.
   - sports you usually play after school or at the weekend
   - what you typically eat before doing sport

   > I usually play basketball after school.

78

Language focus 1 Past simple: *yes/no* questions

1 Complete the examples from the text on page 78.

Yes/No questions	Short answers
Did the sport **start** in China?	Yes, it ..... . No, it **didn't**.

➡ Grammar reference • page 105

2 Complete the questions and answers with the past simple.

A: *Did you go* (you / go) to the football match last night?
B: Yes, I ¹..... .
A: ² ..... (you / sit) with your friends?
B: No, I ³ ..... . I sat with my parents.
A: ⁴ ..... (you / have) a good time?
B: Yes, we ⁵ ..... .
A: ⁶ ..... (your team / win)?
B: No, they ⁷ ..... . They lost.
A: ⁸ ..... (you / eat) after the game?
B: Yes, we ⁹ ..... . We went to a Chinese restaurant.
A: ¹⁰ ..... (your parents / like) the food?
B: Yes, they ¹¹ ..... .

3 Write questions in the past simple.
1. you / go / to a match / last week
   Did you go to a match last week?
2. you / study / last night
3. you / speak English / five years ago
4. your friends / play football / last week
5. it / rain / yesterday
6. your sister / have a shower / three hours ago

Say it right!

In a sentence, we only stress the important words.

a 🔊 **2.24** Listen and repeat.
1. Did you go to the football match last night?
2. Yes, I did.
3. Did your team win?
4. No, they didn't. They lost.

b Mark the stress on the important words in the sentences.
1 Did the sport start in China?
1. Did the sport start in China?
2. No, it didn't. It started in Japan.
3. Did you eat after the game?
4. Yes, we did. We went to a Chinese restaurant.

c 🔊 **2.25** Listen, check and repeat.

Your turn

4 Work with a partner. Ask and answer the questions from Exercise 3.

> Did you go to a tennis match last week?   Yes, I did.

5 Work with a different partner. Ask and answer the questions.
1. The Second World War started in 1929.
2. John Lennon sang with the Beatles.
3. Christopher Columbus discovered Japan.
4. Dinosaurs lived on Earth a hundred years ago.
5. People spoke English in Pompeii in AD79.

> Did the Second World War start in 1929?
>
> No, it didn't. It started in 1939.

Find out about a traditional sports event in Italy.
- How many people went to the Palio?
- When did the Palio start?
- How many riders take part in the Palio?

Discovery EDUCATION

7.1 The Palio

Listening A conversation

1 Do you go to sports events? Which ones do you go to?

2 🔊 2.26 Listen to Vicky and Joe talking about a skateboarding competition. Did Vicky compete?

3 🔊 2.26 Listen again. Which of these things did Vicky do?
1. watched her friend skateboard
2. jumped with a skateboard
3. spent some money
4. bought some clothes
5. bought something for Joe
6. bought a skateboard
7. went to lunch with Dennis
8. ate tacos

Vocabulary Clothes

4 🔊 2.27 Match the pictures with the words. Then listen, check and repeat.

1. a skirt *d*
2. a tracksuit
3. trousers
4. a hoodie
5. a sweatshirt
6. jeans
7. a cap
8. socks
9. a T-shirt
10. boots
11. a jacket
12. shorts

Your turn

5 Ask and answer with your partner.
1. What clothes you are wearing today?
2. What clothes do you wear for your favourite sport?
3. What did you wear yesterday?

> What are you wearing now?

> I'm wearing jeans, a T-shirt …

> What do you wear for basketball?

> I wear …

> What did you wear yesterday?

> I wore my pink T-shirt and …

➡ **Vocabulary bank** • page 113

Language focus 2 Past simple: *Wh-* questions

1 Complete the examples from the listening on page 80.

Wh- question	Answer
…. **did** you **do**?	I went to a skateboard competition.
Who …. you **watch**?	My friend Dennis.
…. **did** you **go**?	We went to a Mexican restaurant.

➡ Grammar reference • page 105

2 Complete the questions with the correct form of the past simple. Use the verbs in brackets.

1 *What did you wear to the game yesterday?*

1 What …. (you / wear) to the game yesterday?
2 When …. (Rick / buy) that hoodie?
3 Who …. (Sarah / play) volleyball with?
4 When …. (the game / end) last night?
5 How many goals …. (we / score)?
6 Who …. (they / go) with last Saturday?

👁 Get it right!

Use *did* with questions in the past simple.
What *did* you do last night? Not ~~What you did last night?~~ ✗

3 Complete the conversation with questions in the past simple.

1 *Where did you buy*

A: Hey, Tom. Where ¹…. your sweatshirt?
B: I bought it online. The Lions are my favourite team. They had a game last night.
A: Cool! Who ²…. ?
B: They played the Tigers.
A: Where ³…. ?
B: They played here. It was a great game!
A: How many ⁴…. ?
B: They scored 20 points. They won the game. We were so excited!
A: We? Who ⁵…. with?
B: I went with my friend Kevin.
A: Oh. Next time maybe I can go with you.
B: OK!

4 🔊 **2.28** Listen and check. Practise the conversation with a partner.

Your turn

5 Use the prompts to write questions about the past. Then ask and answer with a partner.

1 Where / go?
2 When / go?
3 Who / go with?
4 How / get there?
5 What / wear?

> Where did you go last summer?

> I went to a surfing competition.

UNIT 7

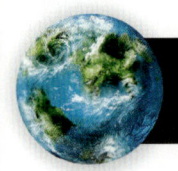

Discover Culture

1 **Look at the pictures. What sport are they playing?**
   a) baseball   b) cricket   c) hockey

2 **Work with a partner. What do you know about the sport they are playing?**

Find out about a cricketer in India.

7.2 The bowler

3 **7.2 Watch the video without sound. Put these things in the order that you see them.**
   1 players wearing normal clothes
   2 a cow and lots of traffic nearby
   3 nets
   4 a trainer
   5 children playing

4 **7.2 Watch the video again with sound. Complete the paragraph with the correct numbers.**
   Cricket is the number ^{1}.... sport in India. It started in England ^{2}.... years ago. Fahim Adin's dream is to be a famous cricket player. He is ^{3}.... years old. When he was a child he played with his ^{4}.... brothers. He can throw the ball over ^{5}.... kilometres per hour!

5 **7.2 Watch the rest of the video. Answer the questions.**
   1 Fahim is a really good bowler. What else is special about him?
   2 How does Fahim communicate?
   3 How well does Fahim play in the important cricket match?
   4 What does the man in picture 5 do?

Your turn

6 **Ask and answer the questions.**
   1 What do you think of cricket?
   2 Would you like to play or watch it Why/Why not?

7 **Who is your sporting hero? Make notes about your favourite sports person.**
   • What sports does he/she play?
   • What makes him/her a good sports person?

8 **Tell your partner about your sporting hero.**

   My sporting hero is ... She won ... She visits schools and ...

Reading   An article

1 Look at the photos. Which country do you think it is? Do you know these sports?

2 🔊 2.29 Read the article. Match the photos with the sports.
1. caber toss
2. stone put
3. hammer throw
4. tug o' war

3 Read the article again. Are the sentences true (*T*) or false (*F*)? Correct the false ones.
1. *F – The Highland Games started in the 19th century.*
1. The Highland Games started this century.
2. There aren't any Highland Games in the winter.
3. King Malcolm was a 19th century king.
4. The winners of the 'heavy' events are strong.
5. People didn't wear tartan in the past.
6. Only Scottish people can compete in the Games.

Explore irregular plurals

4 Find the plurals of these words in the text. Are they regular (*R*) or irregular (*I*)?

~~village~~   man   child   team   person   sport   woman

villages R

➡ **Vocabulary bank** • page 113

Your turn

5 Ask and answer with a partner.
1. Which sport in the text would you like to do? Why?
2. Which sport would you NOT like to do? Why?

> Which sport would you like to do?

> I'd like to do the hammer throw because … What about you?

> I wouldn't like to do … because …

6 Are there any traditional sporting events in your country? What are they?

THE HIGHLAND GAMES

Are you bored with modern sports? Then come to the Highland Games in Scotland and discover traditional Scottish sports. The Games celebrate Scottish culture, and also include Scottish dance competitions and typical local food.

From May to September there are Highland Games in towns and villages across Scotland. Men, women and children travel from all over the world to watch.

Nobody knows when the Games started. But in the 11th century, King Malcolm III of Scotland held a race to find a fast runner to take his messages. Maybe this was the first Highland Games. Some historians say that the Victorians invented The Games in the 19th century.

Competitors at the Games do a lot of different events. There are special 'heavy' athletic sports. One famous event is the *caber toss*. A caber is a heavy wooden pole. Contestants throw the caber. The winners are very strong! Other events are the *stone put* – contestants throw a big stone – and the *hammer throw* – they throw a metal ball on a long stick. Another popular event is the *Tug o' war*. In this event, rival teams pull a rope in opposite directions!

Local Scottish athletes wear traditional tartan kilts similar to skirts. Tartan is a colourful material. In the past, Scottish people wore tartan to show which family they were from.

Nowadays, people from all round the world compete in the events. So why don't you come too and experience the magic of the Highland Games?

FACT! There are Highland Games all round the world. The first Highland Games in the USA took place in New York in 1836.

Speaking Expressing interest

Real Talk: What's your favourite sport and why?

1 ▶ 7.3 Watch the teenagers in the video. Write the sports they talk about.
- baseball
- basketball
- bowling
- cycling
- football
- soccer
- swimming
- table tennis
- tennis
- snowboarding
- volleyball
- windsurfing
- wrestling

2 💬 What's *your* favourite sport and why? Ask and answer with your partner.

3 🔊 2.30 Listen to Max and Rachel talking about the weekend. What did Rachel do?

4 Complete the conversation with the useful language.

Useful language

Cool!   How was it?   Really?   What happened?

Max: What did you do this weekend, **Rachel**?
Rachel: I went **windsurfing** for the first time.
Max: Wow! ¹....
Rachel: It was amazing! But I had problems at first.
Max: Why? ²....
Rachel: I **fell off the board** a lot!
Max: ³....
Rachel: Yeah, but after a few tries, I learned how to do it. I loved it!
Max: ⁴.... It sounds fantastic.
Rachel: It was!

5 🔊 2.30 Listen again and check your answers.

6 💬 Work with a partner. Practise the conversation in Exercise 4.

7 💬 Change the words in bold in the conversation in Exercise 4. Use the information below and your own ideas. Practise the conversation.

Sport	Problem
 bowling	*dropped the ball*
 skiing	*fell down*
 surfing	*fell off the board*

👁 Get it right!

Some words are different in American and British English.

American English	British English
soccer	football
football	American football

Writing A biography

A TEEN ATHLETE

Mohammed Aman was born in Asella, Ethiopia, on January 10, 1994. At the age of 12, he ran at school and was very fast. In 2008, he won his first international race in Nigeria. He won a silver medal at the World Youth Championship in France in 2011 for the 800 metres. In that race, he set a national record. He broke his own record in September that same year. On August 9, he came sixth at the 2012 Olympics in London. At the age of 19, Mohammed won the gold medal at the 2013 World Championships in Moscow. Mohammed wants to go to the next Olympics. We think he'll do really well!

1 Look at the photo. What sport does Mohammed Aman do? Read the biography to check.

2 Write the information in the order it appears in the biography.

> medals and records   his/her future
> place and year of birth   sport(s)

1 ....   2 ....   3 ....   4 ....

3 Read the biography again. What happened at these points in Mohammed's life?

> 2008   the age of 19   2011
> August 9, 2012   January 10, 1994

4 Complete the examples in the Useful language box.

Useful language

Prepositions of time and place
Use the prepositions:
- *on* with dates: .... August 9th
- *in* with months and years: .... December, ... 2014
- *in* with towns/cities and countries: .... London, ... Nigeria
- *at* with sports events and ages: .... the World Championships, ... the age of 12

5 Complete the sentences with the correct prepositions.
1. The diver Qiu Bo was born .... Neijiang, China, ... January 31, 1993.
2. .... the age of five, Karina Petroni started surfing .... Panama.
3. Elvan Can won two silver medals .... the Beijing Olympics .... 2008.
4. Maria Sharapova was born .... Nyagan .... April 19, 1987, but now she lives .... the USA.

Get Writing

PLAN

6 Make notes about someone you know. Use the headings in Exercise 2.

WRITE

7 Write the biography. Use your notes and the language below.
> ... was born in ...
> At the age of ... he/she ...
> After that he/she ...
> In the future he/she ...

CHECK

8 Can you say YES to these questions?
- Have you got information from Exercise 6 in your biography?
- Have you got the correct prepositions of time and place?

8 Holidays

Discovery EDUCATION

In this unit …

- City of water p89
- Alaska p92 
- Going on holiday p94 
- CLIL Holiday in Australia p122 

Vocabulary
- Weather
- Seasons
- Months
- Landscapes
- Collocations 2
- Adjectives

Language focus
- *be going to*
- future with *will/won't*

Unit aims

I can …
- talk about seasons and the weather.
- talk about future intentions.
- ask questions about future intentions.
- understand a conversation about holiday plans.
- talk about landscapes.
- make predictions about the future.
- make suggestions and express preferences.
- write an email about holiday plans.

BE CURIOUS

What can you see in the photo?
Start thinking
- What is the man doing?
- What things do you like doing on holiday?
- What is your ideal holiday?

Vocabulary Seasons and Weather

1 🔊 **2.31** Look at the seasons. Which months are in each season in your country? Then listen and repeat.

January	February
March	April
May	June
July	August
September	October
November	December

spring summer autumn winter

2 🔊 **2.32** Match the photos of the weather with the phrases in the box. Then listen, check and repeat.

> It's sunny.   It's foggy.   ~~It's icy.~~   It's windy.   It's snowy.   It's stormy.   It's rainy.   It's cloudy.

1 *It's icy.*
2 ….
3 ….
4 ….
5 ….
6 ….
7 ….
8 ….

Your turn

3 Complete the table for you.

	Me	My partner
What's your favourite month? Why?	*February. It's my birthday!*	
What's your favourite season? Why?		
What season don't you like? Why not?		

4 Ask and answer the questions with your partner. Complete the table with your partner's information.

➡ Vocabulary bank • page 114

ADVENTURE!

Chloe
I'm going to go on an adventure holiday in Scotland for a week this summer. I'm going to stay in a cabin in the Scottish countryside. There are about 50 different activities: from mountain biking to kayaking in Scottish rivers. My favourite activity is the zip wire. I'm not going to take summer clothes because it's usually quite cold in Scotland, but I don't mind! I can't wait.

Carla
This summer my family and I are going to explore Thailand. We're going to stay in a tree house in the jungle for three days, where we're going to ride elephants. Then we're going to stay in a hotel near the beach for a week. I'm going to swim every day, and we're all going to eat really nice food. Fantastic!

Ivan
My friends and I are going to spend two weeks watching wildlife in Patagonia this summer. We're going to stay in hostels because it's really cheap. Patagonia is a beautiful place in the south of Argentina, with lots of interesting animals. There are penguins, sea lions, even killer whales. I'm going to take my camera, of course, but we aren't going to take our phones. When I get back, my dad's going to build a web page and I'm going to put the best photos on it.

Reading A web page

1. Look at the pictures. Which holiday do you like? Why?

2. 🔊 **2.33** Read the teenagers' posts about their holiday plans. Match each speaker with the correct activity pictures.

3. Read about Chloe, Carla and Ivan's holiday plans again. Who has plans to …
   1. go on holiday for a week?
   2. stay in more than one place?
   3. stay in the countryside?
   4. travel with friends?
   5. do activities on water?
   6. go on holiday with family?

Explore collocations

4. Look at the expressions in the table. Copy and complete the table with similar expressions to the ones in the text.

Stay	Spend	Take
in a hostel	a day	a bike
	a month	

➡ **Vocabulary bank** • page 114

Your turn

5. Make notes about your last holiday.
   - where you stayed
   - what you did
   - how long you spent there
   - what you took

6. Tell your partner about your last holiday.

   > I went to Paris last year.

Language focus 1 *be going to*

1 Complete the examples from the text on page 88.

	I	He / She / It	We / You / They
+	I .... **swim** every day.	My dad .... **build** a web page.	We .... **explore** Thailand.
–	I**'m not going to take** summer clothes.	She i**sn't going to come** with us.	We .... **take** our mobile phones.
?	**Am** I **going to build** a web page?	**Is** he **going to ride** an elephant?	Where **are** you **going to stay**?

➡ Grammar reference • page 106

2 Complete the sentences with the correct form of *be*.
1 I **'m** going to take lots of photos. (✓)
2 My classmates and I .... going to study hard for our English exam. (✓)
3 They .... going to stay in a hotel in the countryside. (✗)
4 My mother .... going to cook when we're on holiday. (✗)
5 My sister and her best friend .... going to cycle to the south of France. (✓)

3 Write questions with *be going to*.
1 *Is he going to play football on Saturday?*
1 he / play / football on Saturday?
2 you / watch / TV tonight?
3 what / you / watch?
4 when / they / do / their homework?
5 where / we / go / on holiday this year?

4 Match the questions in Exercise 3 with the correct answers.
1 *d*
a) At the weekend.
b) A film.
c) Scotland.
d) No, he isn't.
e) Yes, we are.

Your turn

5 Change the questions in Exercise 3. Ask and answer with your partner.
Are you going to play football this weekend?

Yes, I am. No, I'm not.

6 Write six true sentences about your partner.
1 *Maria isn't going to play football this weekend.*

Say it right!

going to
In informal English, we sometimes pronounce *going to* as 'gonna' (/gənə/).

🔊 **2.34** Listen and repeat.
1 /gənə/ What are you going to do?
2 /gənə/ I'm going to take a lot of photos.

7 Work with a partner. Ask and answer the questions in Exercise 5. Use the informal 'gonna'.

Find out about the popular tourist destination of Venice.
• How many cars are there in Venice?
• How do people travel in Venice?
• What do people wear for Carnevale?

Discovery EDUCATION
8.1 City of water

Listening A conversation

1. Look at the photos. What country do you think they show? Which do you like best? Why?

2. 🔊 **2.35** Listen to the conversation between Chloe and Ivan. Which of the places in the photos do they NOT talk about?

3. 🔊 **2.35** Listen again. Are the sentences true (*T*) or false (*F*)?
   1. Chloe is worried about the weather in Scotland. ....
   2. Chloe is going to visit Scotland in the winter. ....
   3. Chloe isn't going to take many photos in Scotland. ....
   4. Ivan is going to travel with his friends to Patagonia. ....
   5. Chloe thinks Ivan is a good photographer. ....
   6. Carla didn't enjoy her holiday in Thailand very much. ....

Vocabulary Landscapes

4. Look at the photos in Exercise 1. Find the landscape words below. Which words aren't in the photos?

   > mountains   sea   lake   beach
   > river   jungle   desert   hill   forest

5. 🔊 **2.36** Listen and repeat.

Your turn

6. Choose a holiday destination. Make notes about it. Say why you want to go there.
   There are a lot of mountains and beaches in California.

7. Ask your partner about their holiday destination. Try to guess where it is.

   > Are there mountains there? Why do you want to go there? Is it America?

➡ Vocabulary bank • page 114

Language focus 2 Future with *will/won't*

1 Complete the examples from the listening on page 90.

	I / You / He / She / It / We / They
+	I think I' …. **take** my camera.
–	Maybe I …. **go** to Scotland next year!
?	What …. the weather **be** like?

➡ **Grammar reference** • page 106

2 Complete the sentences with the correct form of *will* and the verb in brackets.
1. My teacher thinks we <u>will do</u> (do) well in the test.
2. The weather …. (not be) very nice tomorrow.
3. You …. (have) a great time in Patagonia!
4. They …. (not see) any penguins at this time of year.
5. My dad says I …. (not enjoy) kayaking.

3 Complete the email with *will* and the verbs below.

> walk   have   not rain   leave   make   like

✉

I'm very happy that you're going to come camping with me this weekend. I think we ¹ …. a great time!

Come to my house on Saturday morning. My mum ² …. some breakfast for us. She's a great cook – I'm sure you ³ …. her food.

I think we ⁴ …. the house at about 10 o'clock. The campsite isn't far, so we ⁵ …. there. The weather forecast says it ⁶ …., and I'm very glad about that!

See you on Saturday!
Dave

▶ Kirstie

Your turn

4 Write sentences about the future using a prompt from each box.

> go to my friend's house
> go to university   get a job
> have a shower   have a snack
> go swimming   buy a house

> after school today   when I leave school
> when I'm older   this afternoon
> tomorrow   next week

1 *I think I'll go to my friend's house after school today.*

1. I think … .
2. I hope … .
3. I'm sure … .
4. I don't think … .
5. … .
6. … .
7. … .

5 Work with a partner. Make questions from the sentences in Exercise 4. Ask extra information questions when the answer is *yes*.

> Will you go to your friend's house after school today?

> Yes, I will.

> What do you think you'll do there?

Discover Culture

1 Look at the map. Which country is next to Alaska? Which country is Alaska part of? What else do you know about Alaska?

2 Match the extreme sports to the pictures.
   1 snowboarding   2 bungee jumping   3 parachuting   4 kayaking

3 Which of the things do you think you'll see in the video?

> a beach   icebergs   a house   a volcano   a river
> a mountain top   the Northern Lights   skiing   a glacier

Find out about adventure holidays in Alaska.

8.2 Alaska

4 **8.2** Watch the first part of the video (up to 0.38) without sound and check your answers.

5 **8.2** Watch the video with sound. Complete the paragraph with the words below.

> mountains   exciting   a lot of   snowy
> ~~adventure~~   sports   cold

Alaska is great for people who like ¹ _adventure_ and very ² …. weather. It is a very ³ …. place to be. There are ⁴ …. things to do, including extreme ⁵ …. . They have really spectacular ⁶ …. landscapes. Alaska is amazing, the ⁷ …. are incredible, the views are beautiful. Come on an adventure here!

6 Find six positive adjectives in the text.

7 **8.2** Watch the video again. Write the sports in the order you would most like to do them.

Your turn

8 Work with a partner. Would you like to try any of these extreme sports? Which ones? Why? / Why not?

> I'd like to try snowboarding but I can't, there are no mountains here.

> Me too. I'd like to try …

9 What other extreme sports do you know? Which one(s) would you like to try?

10 Why do people come to your country on holiday? Think about the weather, the landscapes, the culture, the food, etc. Write a list. Then work with a partner and compare your ideas.

> I think people come to … on holiday because they like the culture.

SUMMER ⛺ CAMP!

UNIT 8

In the USA there is a tradition of sending teenagers to summer camps while the parents stay at home. Every year over 11 million children and teenagers go to one of these. They are very popular because there are a lot of fun activities to do. They usually last two or three weeks. There are a lot of different kinds of camps. Here are some examples. Which do you like best?

A .... Our two-week camp is a perfect introduction to the 'Land of the Midnight Sun'. You'll go sea kayaking, sailing, snowboarding and camping and you'll learn about the history of the region and the animals that live here.

B .... Join other musicians for two weeks of musical fun. You'll improve your skills during the day in classes with great teachers. Then every evening you'll relax at a special concert or at a party on the beach. Other activities are sports, board games and drama.

C .... Learn new skills this summer at the University of Colorado – web design, game design; everything you want to know about computers. You'll stay in university rooms and use the amazing technology that our students use.

D .... A camp for everyone from great athletes to complete beginners. We train hard every day, and at night you'll be very tired! But you'll have fun and play lots of new sports for the first time. You'll sleep well in our luxury cabins in the beautiful mountains of Virginia.

E .... Do you love horses? Do you know how to ride? This is the summer camp for you. You'll get your own horse for the two-week course and you'll learn all about how to take care of it. At the end of this holiday you'll be an excellent horse rider and you won't want to leave!

Reading   A holiday brochure

1 Look at the pictures on this page. What activities can you see?

2 What kind of holiday is the brochure describing? Read the brochure and match the titles with the descriptions A–E.
  1 Florida summer band camp
  2 Riding camp
  3 Alaskan adventure camp
  4 Super summer sports camp
  5 Tech camp Colorado

3 🔊 2.37 Read the text again. In which places will you …
  1 see animals?
  2 work very hard?
  3 stay at a university?
  4 already know how to do the main activity?
  5 do watersports?
  6 be near the sea?

Explore adjectives

4 What do these adjectives describe? Read the text again and check your answers.

> popular   perfect   special   amazing   luxury   excellent

➡ **Vocabulary bank** • page 114

Your turn

5 Compare a typical summer holiday of yours with the summer camps you read about here. Make a list of how many ways they are different.
We don't usually go on holiday without our parents.

6 Work with a partner. Listen to your partner's descriptions and report to the class.

> Xanthe doesn't usually go on holiday without her parents.

Speaking Making suggestions

Real Talk: Where do you like going on holiday?

1. ▶ 8.3 Watch the teenagers in the video. Write down the places that they talk about.
   - Florida
   - Ireland
   - Turkey
   - Scotland
   - Canada
   - Barbados

2. 💬 Where do *you* like going on holiday? Ask and answer with your partner.

3. 🔊 2.38 Listen to Mia and Rose talking about their summer holiday. Who doesn't want to go on a summer camp?

4. Complete the conversation with the useful language.

5. 🔊 2.38 Listen again and check your answers.

6. 💬 Work with a partner. Practise the conversation in Exercise 4.

7. 💬 Change the words in bold in the conversation in Exercise 4. Use the information below. Your partner thinks of a reason why he/she doesn't want to go on that holiday.

Useful language

Let's   What about   Why don't we   I'd prefer
do you want to go   That's a good idea!

Mia:	Where ¹.... on holiday this year, Rose?
Rose:	².... going **on a summer camp**?
Mia:	A summer camp? ³.... not to go to summer camp.
Rose:	Why not?
Mia:	⁴.... go somewhere hot, like **Portugal**.
Rose:	Yes, that'll be nice. There's a lot to do in **Portugal**.
Mia:	We can go **surfing, water skiing, swimming**.
Rose:	⁵....! Do you think Dad will agree?
Mia:	⁶.... ask him.

ITALY
WINTER HOLIDAY

WHERE:
Cortina, Dolomites

WHAT:
skiing, snowboarding, ice-skating

SCOTLAND
ADVENTURE HOLIDAY

WHERE:
Dundee

WHAT:
horse riding, kayaking, mountain biking

> Where shall we go on holiday this year?

> What about going on this winter holiday in Italy?

> I'd prefer not …

Writing An email

1 Look at the photo and read Simon's email. How many places is he going to visit in Brazil?

> Paula ▶
>
> Hi Paula
>
> Thanks for your email. The photos of your dog are great! I'm going to show them to my mum – she'll love them!
>
> Guess what? I'm going to visit Brazil for a month! I'm going to go with my parents, my sister and my granddad. I can't wait. We're going to fly to Rio first. We're going to stay with Dad's friend, Cristiano. Then we'll drive south to a city called Paraty and we'll go to the beach there. It'll be very relaxing after Rio, because there won't be so many people. We'll stay there for a week I think. Have you got any holiday plans?
>
> Write again soon,
> Simon
>
> Simon ▶

2 Read Simon's email again. What are his answers to these questions?
1. Where are you going to go?
2. Who are you going to go with?
3. How are you going to travel?
4. Where are you going to stay?
5. What are you going to do?
6. How long will you be there?

Useful language

Starting and finishing an email

Start	Finish
Thanks for your message. How are you? I hope you are well. ….	Please write soon. Speak soon. Looking forward to hearing from you. ….

3 How does Simon start and finish his email? Put the phrases in the correct column above.

Get Writing

PLAN

4 Make notes about your next holiday. Include information from Exercise 2.
Where …
Who …
How …
What …
How long …

WRITE

5 Write an email to a friend. Use your notes from Exercise 4, and the language below.
We're going to visit …
We're going to fly/drive …
We'll stay there for …

CHECK

6 Can you say YES to these questions?
- Have you got information from Exercise 4 in your email?
- Do you start and finish the email with an expression from the Useful language box?
- Are your spelling, grammar and vocabulary correct?

7–8 Review

Vocabulary

1 Write the names of the sports. Include the verbs.
1 *go swimming*

2 Write the names of the clothes in the picture.
1 *cap*

3 Match the months with the seasons.
1 spring   a) December, January, February
2 summer   b) September, October, November
3 autumn   c) June, July, August
4 winter   d) March, April, May

4 Match the pictures with the words.
1 *d*

1 cloudy	4 rainy	7 sunny
2 foggy	5 snowy	8 windy
3 icy	6 stormy	

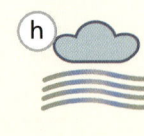

5 Complete the sentences with the words in the box.

> beach   desert   forest   hill   sea   mountain

1 They're swimming in the *sea*.
2 It's hot and dry. We're in the …. .
3 Let's sit on the …. and look at the sea.
4 It's easy to walk up this …. . It's not very high.
5 There are a lot of tall trees. We're in a …. .
6 It's hard to climb up this because it's very high. It's a …. .

6 Choose the best words to complete the text.

Last summer I ¹…. two weeks at a summer camp in the United States. Summer camps are very ²…. there, and a lot of teenagers ³…. go on one every year. It was my first time, and I thought it was ⁴…. . I ⁵…. in a ⁶…. cabin with four other kids my age. It was ⁷…. comfortable. I ⁸…. my computer and a camera with me, and sent photos back to my parents. We ⁹…. every day doing lots of fun activities, and I was sad to come home because it was a really ¹⁰…. holiday.

1 a) spent   b) took
2 a) perfect   b) popular
3 a) usually   b) surprisingly
4 a) popular   b) amazing
5 a) stayed   b) spent
6 a) little   b) perfect
7 a) traditionally   b) surprisingly
8 a) took   b) stayed
9 a) spent   b) took
10 a) special   b) luxury

7 Write the plurals of the words. Which ones are regular / irregular?
1 man   4 girl
2 baby   5 child
3 woman   6 person

Language focus

1 Complete the sentences with the words in the box.

> didn't (x2)   Did   Yes

1 .... Susan play tennis yesterday?
2 A: Did you go snowboarding last winter?
  B: ...., I did.
3 A: Did Tom go with you on holiday?
  B: No, he .....
4 A: Did they have a good time?
  B: No, they .....

2 Write the questions.

1 A: Where *did you go*?
  B: I went to the shopping centre.
2 A: Who ....?
  B: I went with Jamie.
3 A: What ....?
  B: I bought a hoodie.
4 A: How much ....?
  B: It cost £9.99.

3 Complete the conversation with the correct form of *be going to*.

1 *are you going to do*

Owen:	What ¹(you / do) when you leave school?
Alex:	²(I / go) to university, but first ³(I / take) a year out and travel around Europe.
Owen:	Cool! ⁴(I / try) and get a job. ⁵(I / not go) to university. Who ⁶(you / go travelling) with?
Alex:	My cousin. ⁷(We / start) in the north, in Scandinavia, and finish in the south in Spain and go to all of the countries in between.
Owen:	Wow! That's a lot of countries.
Alex:	What about you? ⁸(you / travel) in the future?
Owen:	Maybe! Your trip sounds great!

4 Match the sentences, then write the correct form of *will* and the verb in brackets.

1 Don't forget your umbrella. *a*
2 Sonya studies very hard.
3 You didn't do your homework!
4 I made a cake for you.
5 Let's take the children to Disneyland.

a) I think it *'ll rain* (rain) later today.
b) Everyone says she .... (pass) her exams easily.
c) They .... (love) it!
d) Your teacher .... (not be) happy about that.
e) I hope you .... (like) it.

Language builder

UNIT 7–8

5 Choose the correct words to complete the text.

1 *a*

Dear Antonio,
Here is a photo of my home town. It's a very nice place. 500 years ¹...., it ²... very small. Today there are over 100,000 people. You ³... travel around town by bus or by tram, but there isn't an underground – they're ⁴... one in a few years! Last year, we ⁵... a big football tournament here. My team ⁶... in the final match! But we ⁷... win. Next year, the town ⁸... a festival of culture. They are building a lot of new hotels because visitors from a lot of countries ⁹... visit us. You must come and visit me one day. You ¹⁰... stay with me and my family.
Best wishes,
Gino

	a	b	c
1	ago	was	it does
2	are	were	was
3	can	will	won't
4	built	going to build	build
5	have	had	did have
6	play	playing	played
7	not	doesn't	didn't
8	is going to have	is have	had
9	is going	are going to	is going to
10	can	going	don't

Speaking

6 Complete the conversation with the words in the box.

> That's a good idea   ~~Let's~~   I'd prefer   Really
> What about   Cool   What happened

Tim:	¹ *Let's* go kayaking this weekend.
Karla:	² .... not to go kayaking.
Tim:	Why not?
Karla:	I went last year.
Tim:	³ ....?
Karla:	Yes, really.
Tim:	⁴ ....!
Karla:	It wasn't. I didn't enjoy it at all.
Tim:	⁵ ....?
Karla:	I spent a lot of time in the water and not much time in the kayak.
Tim:	Oh. OK. ⁶ .... going to the cinema instead?
Karla:	⁷ .... Shall we go tomorrow afternoon?
Tim:	Yes, OK.

Grammar reference

Starter Unit

Subject pronouns and *be*: affirmative, negative and questions

subject pronoun	+ full form	contraction	− full form	contraction
I	I am	I'm	I am not	I'm not
You	You are	You're	You are not	You aren't
He	He is	He's	He is not	He isn't
She	She is	She's	She is not	She isn't
It	It is	It's	It is not	It isn't
We	We are	We're	We are not	We aren't
You	You are	You're	You are not	You aren't
They	They are	They're	They are not	They aren't

- Use the present simple of *be* to identify people and give locations and dates.
  He's my uncle.
  They're in the house.
  It's the 12th March.
- You can use subject pronouns instead of names to refer to people or things. You can use contractions to combine subject pronouns with the present simple of *be*.
  Millie's my friend.
  She's my friend.
- Change the word order to make questions; put *be* before the subject.

?	short answers +	−
Am I at school?	Yes, I am.	No, I'm not.
Are you at school?	Yes, you are.	No, you aren't.
Is he/she/it at school?	Yes, he/she/it is.	No, he/she/it isn't.
Are we/you/they at school?	Yes, we/you/they are.	No, we/you/they aren't.

1 Complete the conversations with the correct subject pronouns and the present simple of the verb *be*. Use contractions where possible.

1. **A:** Is Lara 18?
   B: No, *she isn't*. *She's* 19.
2. **A:** Are Tim and Ella students?
   B: Yes, ………… in my class.
3. **A:** …… you in the basketball team?
   B: No ………… in the football team.
4. **A:** …… I in Room C?
   B: No, you're not. …… in Room D.

Possessive adjectives and possessive *'s*

singular	plural
my/your/his/her/its	our/your/their

- We use possessive adjectives to talk about possession.
  This is my computer.
- We use *his* for boys and men and *her* for girls and women.
  His name's Tom.
  Her name's Amanda.
- We use the possessive adjective *its* for animals and things.
  My dog is black but its feet are white.
- We use *apostrophe + s* to show possession.
- We put *'s* after a name or singular noun and *s'* after a plural noun.

2 Write the sentences two ways. Use possessive *'s* and possessive adjectives.

1. Lydia / shoes are blue.
   Lydia's shoes are blue. Her shoes are blue.
2. The dog / ball is red.
3. The teachers / names are Mr Lark and Mrs Moore.
4. Andrew / parents are from Chile.

Grammar reference

Unit 1

Have got: affirmative and negative

+	I've got	
	You've got	
	He/She/It 's got	a sister.
	We've got	
	You've got	
	They've got	
–	I haven't got	
	You haven't got	
	He/She/It hasn't got	a brother.
	We haven't got	
	You haven't got	
	They haven't got	

- We use *have (not/n't) got* to talk about possession.
I've got a brother.
I haven't got a sister.

Have got: questions and short answers

?	Have I/we/you/they got	a skateboard?
?	Has he/she/it got	
+	Yes, I/we/you/they	have.
+	Yes, he/she/it	has.
–	No, I/we/you/they	haven't.
–	No, he/she/it	hasn't.

- We use *have + subject + got + object* to make questions.
Have you got a skateboard?
- We use short answers when we speak.
A: Have you got a skateboard?
B: Yes, I have. / No, I haven't.

1 Write affirmative (✓) or negative (✗) sentences with *have got*.
1 She / two cousins. (✓)
She's got two cousins.
2 I / blue eyes. (✓)
3 Harry / a pencil. (✓)
4 You / a bike. (✗)
5 We / a big garden. (✗)
6 My grandparents / mobile phones. (✓)

2 Write six questions and short answers for the sentences in Exercise 1.
Has she got two cousins?
Yes, she has. / No she hasn't.

Comparative adjectives

1 syllable	dark → dark**er**	My hair is darker than his hair.
	nice → nic**er**	James is nicer than Megan.
	big → big**ger**	My brother is bigger than your brother.
	tall → tall**er**	She's taller than me.
2 or more syllables	intelligent → **more** intelligent	My avatar is more intelligent than yours.
	beautiful → **more** beautiful	My cat's more beautiful than yours.
	good-looking → **more** good-looking	My brother's more good-looking than Robert Pattinson.
Ending in consonant + -y	funny → funn**ier**	This film's funnier than that film.
	happy → happ**ier**	Lara is happier than Sara.
Irregular	good → **better**	Ahmed's phone's better than my phone.
	bad → **worse**	My phone's worse than his phone.
	far → **further**	America is further from the UK than France.

- We use comparative adjectives to show how two things are different from each other.

3 Write sentences with comparative adjectives.
1 Bella / old / her sister.
Bella is older than her sister.
2 Mark / tall / Ben.
3 My hair / curly / my mum's hair.
4 Oliver / handsome / his brother.
5 Our avatar / bad / her avatar.

4 Write sentences. Compare these things.
Your country and the USA.
My country is smaller than the USA.
You and your friend.
Your hair and your teacher's hair.
Your family and your friend's family.
Your town and another town.

Grammar reference

Unit 2
Present simple: affirmative and negative

+	I/We/You/They	live	in Ankara.
-		don't live	
+	He/She/It	lives	
-		doesn't live	

- We use the present simple to talk about facts, habits and routines.
  She doesn't speak French.
  He goes to football on Mondays.
- We form the negative of the present simple with **subject + don't/doesn't + infinitive**
  They don't speak English. She doesn't eat eggs.

1 Complete the sentences with the affirmative (✓) or negative (✗) form of the verbs in brackets.
  1 I ..*don't live*.. (✗) in Paris. I ..*live*.. (✓) in New York. (live)
  2 He …. (✗) lunch at school. He …. (✓) lunch at home. (have)
  3 I …. (✓) early on week days, but I …. (✗) early at the weekend. (get up)
  4 Sarah …. (✗) skateboarding in her garden. She …. (✓) skateboarding in the park. (go)
  5 You …. (✗) basketball on Tuesday. You …. (✓) on Thursday. (play)

Spelling: third person

- The third person form of the present simple ends in –s.
  eat – he eats   read – she reads   live – it lives
- When the verb ends in **consonant + y**, we change the *y* and add *–ies* in the third person.
  carry – he carries   fly – she flies
- When the verb ends in *–ss, –sh, –ch, –x* and *–o*, we add *–es*.
  she finishes   he relaxes   it goes
- Some verbs have an irregular third person:
  have – has   be – is

2 Write the third person form of the following verbs.
  write ….   fix ….
  marry ….   do ….
  watch ….   be ….

Adverbs of frequency

always   usually   often   sometimes   never
100%   0%

- We use adverbs of frequency to say how often we do something. They go after the verb *be* but before the main verb.
  She's always happy.   He never smiles.

3 Put the adverb of frequency in the correct place.
  1 They *always* listen to music at weekends. *always*
  2 Liz and Dave are late. *often*
  3 We watch TV in the morning. *never*
  4 My dog is happy. *always*
  5 You work hard at school. *usually*

Present simple: Yes/No questions and short answers.

?	Do	I/we/you/they	live in Ankara?
?	Does	he/she/it	
+	Yes,	I/we/you/they	do.
		he/she/it/	does.
-	No,	I/we/you/they	don't.
		he/she/it	doesn't.

- We form present simple *yes/no* questions with **Do/Does + subject + infinitive.**
  A: Do you live in Turkey?   B: Yes, I do. / No, I don't.

Present simple: Wh- questions

question word	do/does	subject	verb
Who	do	I/you	know?
What time		the party	start?
Where	does	she	live?
What		he	do?
When	do	we/you/they	have supper?

- We form *Wh-* questions with **question word + do/does + subject + verb**.
  What time do you get up?

4 Complete the questions with the correct question word and *do/does*.
  1 …. you go to dance class?
  2 …. Mari live?
  3 …. your little sisters go to bed?
  4 …. you walk to school with?

100 Grammar reference

Grammar reference

Unit 3

can for ability and permission

+	I/You/He/She/It/We/They	can	sing.
–	I/You/He/She/It/We/They	can't	

?	Can	I/you/she/it/we/they	sing?
+	Yes,	I/you/he/she/it/we/they	can.
–	No,	I/you/he/she/it/we/they	can't.

- We use *can* to express ability and permission.
  He can play tennis. (ability)
  Dad says we can't go to the party. (permission)
- *Can* is the same in all forms.
  I can speak Chinese.
  She can speak Chinese.
- We use *infinitive* without *to* after *can*.
  They can sing.
- We don't use *do/does* when we make questions with *can*.
  Can you use your mobile phone at school?

1 Write affirmative (✓) and negative (✗) sentences with *can*.

1. Jamie / run fast. (✓)
   Jamie can run fast.
2. My granddad / use a mobile phone. (✓)
3. They / skateboard. (✗)
4. You / stay out late tonight. (✗)
5. I / ski. (✗)
6. She / play the piano. (✓)

2 Write questions and short answers for the sentences in Exercise 1.
Can Jamie run fast?   Yes, he can. / No, he can't.

3 Write sentences with *can* about you and your friends and family. Use the prompts to help.

1. play the guitar / piano
   I can play the guitar. I can't play the piano, but my uncle can.
2. swim / dance / ride a bike / ride a horse
3. speak French / Russian / Chinese / Spanish
4. drive a car / drive a lorry / fly a plane

love, (don't) like, don't mind, hate + -ing

- We use the *-ing* form of the verb after *love, (don't) like* and *hate*.
  She loves playing with her little sister.
  I don't mind doing homework.

4 Complete the sentences with the *-ing* form of the verbs in the box.

do   walk   go   paint   sing   watch   play   learn

1. He loves …. to school.
2. I don't like …. homework.
3. Karen loves …. DVDs.
4. We like …. English.
5. They don't like …. pictures.
6. He doesn't mind …. with the baby.
7. My brother hates ….
8. They don't mind …. to school.

Object pronouns

subject pronoun	I	you	he	she	it	we	you	they
object pronoun	me	you	him	her	it	us	you	them

- We can use object pronouns to replace nouns that follow verbs.
  I love Maths lessons. → *I love them.*
  I don't like cooking. → *I don't like it.*

5 Complete the sentences with the correct object pronoun.

1. Our teacher always tells <u>us</u> to sit down.
2. It's a great film. Watch …. !
3. She's got exams. She needs to study for ….
4. Brad goes to Art classes. I can go with ….
5. Katia knows the answer. I can email …. tomorrow.
6. My best friend always tells …. her secrets.

Grammar reference

Unit 4

Countable and uncountable nouns

- Most nouns are countable. They have singular and plural forms.
  one girl – two girls   one car – two cars
- Some nouns are uncountable. They don't have a plural form.
  bread, milk, homework, music

a/an, some and any

	singular countable	plural countable	uncountable
+	I've got an orange.	I've got some potatoes.	I've got some pasta.
–	I haven't got an orange.	I haven't got any potatoes.	I haven't got any pasta.
?	Have you got an orange?	Have you got any potatoes?	Have you got any pasta?

- We use *a* with singular countable nouns, or *an* when the noun starts with a vowel.
  a banana   a dog   a guitar
  an orange   an elephant   an egg
- We use *some* and *any* with plural countable nouns and uncountable nouns when we don't know how much there is of something or it's not important. We usually use *some* for affirmative sentences and *any* for negative sentences and questions.
  I've got some apples and some bread.
  I haven't got any bananas or any pasta.
  Have we got any oranges? Have we got any cheese?

1 Complete the sentences with *a/an*, *some* or *any*.

1. We've got …. red car.
2. I've got …. bananas.
3. Ana doesn't like …. fruit.
4. Can I have …. orange, please?
5. They haven't got …. biscuits.
6. Have you got …. green pen?

there is / there are

	singular	plural
+	There's a supermarket.	There are some chips on the tray.
–	There isn't a supermarket.	There aren't any chips on
?	Is there a supermarket?	Are there any chips?
+	Yes, there is.	Yes, there are.
–	No, there isn't.	No, there aren't.

- We use *there is* (*there's*) with singular countable and uncountable nouns.
  There's a cinema.   There's some cheese.
- We use *there are* with plural countable nouns.
  There are four pizzas.
- In questions and negatives we use *any* with plural and uncountable nouns.
  Is there any milk?   There aren't any books.

2 Use the information to write questions and short answers about the two places.

	Hessle	Cottingham
a sports centre	✗	✓
good restaurants	✓	✗
a cinema	✗	✓

Is there a sports centre in Hessle? No, there isn't.

much / many / a lot of

	countable plural	uncountable
+	There are a lot of apples.	There's a lot of cheese.
–	There aren't many apples.	There isn't much cheese.
?	How many apples are there?	How much cheese is there?

- We use *much*, *many* and *a lot of* to talk about quantity.
- We use *much* in negative sentences with uncountable nouns and *many* in negative sentences with countable nouns.
  There isn't much milk and there aren't many apples.
- We use *a lot of* in affirmative sentences to describe a large quantity of something.
  There are a lot of apples and there's a lot of meat.
- We use *how much/many* to ask about quantity.
  How many sisters have you got?
  How much money have you got?

3 Complete the sentences with *much*, *many* or *a lot of*.

1. How ..*many*.. students are there in your class?
   There are 35.
2. Has Jenny got any good DVDs?
   Yes, she's got …. good DVDs.
3. There isn't …. orange juice – only one bottle!
4. Are there any shops in your town?
   Yes, there are …. shops.
5. How …. pasta can you eat?

Grammar reference

Unit 5
Present continuous: affirmative and negative

+	I	am	
	He/She/It	is	
	We/You/They	are	running.
−	I	'm not	
	He/She/It	isn't	
	We/You/They	aren't	

- We use the present continuous to talk about actions in progress at the time of speaking.
  We're learning English. I'm reading this book.
- We form the present continuous with *subject + be (not/n't) + verb + ing*.
  He's laughing. He isn't crying.

Spelling: *-ing* form
- With most verbs, we add *-ing* to the verb.
  eat – eating
- Verbs that end in *-e*, remove the *-e* and add *-ing*.
  write – writing
- Verbs that end in a vowel and a consonant, double the final consonant and add *-ing*.
  stop – stopping

1 Write the *-ing* form of the verbs.

1 run ...*running*... 4 play ....
2 help ....   5 write ....
3 stop ....   6 swim ....

2 Write affirmative and negative sentences in the present continuous.

1 He / read / a comic. (✓)
   He's reading a comic.
2 They / listen / to us. (✗)
3 Laura / do / her homework. (✓)
4 He / work / on this exercise. (✗)
5 We / go / to our Art class. (✓)
6 Joe / eat / his lunch. (✗)

3 Re-write the sentences in Exercise 2 so they are true for you.

I'm not reading a comic.

Present continuous: questions and short answers

? (What)	am	I	
	is	he/she/it	writing?
	are	we/you/they	
+ Yes,	I am.		
	he/she/it is.		
	we/you/they are.		
− No,	I'm not.		
	he/she/it isn't.		
	we/you/they aren't.		

- To form *yes/no* questions, we use *be + -ing*. To give a short answer, we don't use the verb + *-ing*.
  Are you listening? Yes, I am. / No, I'm not.
- For *Wh-* questions, we put the question word before *be*.
  Where are you going? What are you doing?

Present simple and present continuous
- We use the present simple to talk about facts, habits and routines.
- We use the present continuous to talk about actions in progress at the time of speaking.
  I read a lot of comics. At the moment, I'm reading Superman!
- We use adverbs of frequency with the present simple. We use *at the moment* and *now* with the present continuous.

4 Complete the questions and short answers.

1 ...*Am*... I ...*helping*...? (help) (✓) *Yes, you are.*
2 .... he .... ? (smile) (✓)
3 .... they .... ? (dance) (✗)
4 .... she .... her teeth? (brush) (✗)
5 .... they .... dinner? (have) (✓)

5 Complete the sentences with the present simple or present continuous.

1 We *go* swimming on Friday. (go)
2 I .... to the football. It's 2–1! (listen)
3 When .... you .... your friends? (see)
4 .... you .... French? (understand)
5 It ...., but I don't want to go out. (not rain)
6 I can't see you! Where .... you .... ? (hide)

Grammar reference

Unit 6

was/were: affirmative, negative, questions and short answers

+	I/He/She/It	was	hungry.
	We/You/They	were	
−	I/He/She/It	wasn't	
	We/You/They	weren't	

?	Was	I/he/she/it	hungry?
	Were	we/you/they	
+	Yes,	I/he/she/it	was.
		we/you/they	were.
−	No,	I/he/she/it	wasn't.
		we/you/they	weren't.

- *Was* and *were* are the past simple forms of *be*.
  The door was red and the windows were green.
- To form *yes/no* questions, we use *was/were* before the subject. We don't use *do*.
  Was the door blue? Were the windows red?
- To form *Wh-* questions, we put the question word before *was/were*.
  What colour was the car? Where were you yesterday?

1 Choose the correct words.

1. She **was** / **were** here at 8 am.
2. We **wasn't** / **weren't** at the cinema.
3. Why **was** / **were** Javier and Daniel late?
4. I **was** / **were** at school yesterday.
5. Where **were** / **was** you at 9.30?

2 Write questions with was/were. Answer them with short answers.

1. your dad / with you? (✗)
   Was your dad with you? No, he wasn't.
2. the film / good? (✓)
3. you / at home / at 8 pm? (✗)
4. the city centre / busy / on Saturday? (✓)
5. they / at the bowling alley / last night? (✓)

there was/were: affirmative, negative, questions and short answers

	Singular	Plural
+	There was a cinema here in the 1950s.	There were three shops here.
−	There wasn't a cinema here in the 1950s.	There weren't any shops here.

	Singular	Plural
?	Was there a cinema here in the 1950s?	Were there any shops?
+	Yes, there was.	Yes, there were.
−	No, there wasn't.	No, there weren't.

- *There was* and *there were* are the past simple forms of *there is* and *there are*.
  There was a park and there were houses next to it.

Past simple regular verbs

+	I/You/He/She/It/We/They	played football yesterday.
−	I/You/He/She/It/We/They	didn't play football yesterday.

- We use the past simple to talk about completed events and actions in the past.
  I tidied my room yesterday.
- We add *-ed* to regular verbs to form the past tense.
  walk – walked
- When a verb ends in *-y*, we take off the *y* and add *ied*.
  tidy – tidied

Past simple irregular verbs: affirmative and negative

- Some verbs are irregular in the past simple. They don't follow any pattern. (See page 126)
- We form the negative of the past simple with *subject + didn't + infinitive*

3 Complete the sentences with the past simple form of the verbs in the box.

> escape   ~~walk~~   start   live   stay

1. We ..*walked*.. to school this morning.
2. The class …. at 4.30.
3. Twenty years ago, my parents …. in Spain.
4. Last summer, we …. at my grandparents' house.
5. Last week, a lion …. from the zoo.

ago

- We use *ago* with the past simple and a period of time to talk about when something happened in the past.
  I went to the USA a year ago. He arrived an hour ago.

4 Put the words in the correct order to make sentences.

1. saw / two weeks / I / him / ago
2. two years / stayed / aunt / at my house / ago / my
3. the cup / ago / My team / won / ten years
4. ago / my homework / did / half an hour / I
5. our class project / finished / We / ago / four days

Grammar reference

Unit 7

Past simple: questions and short answers

?	Did	I/he/she/it/we/you/they	walk to school?
+	Yes,	I/he/she/it/we/you/they	did.
–	No,	I/he/she/it/we/you/they	didn't.

- We form past simple questions with *did + subject + infinitive*
  Did she enjoy the party?
  Yes, she did. / No, she didn't.
- We form *Wh-* questions in the past simple with *question word + did + subject + infinitive*
  What did you do at the weekend?

1 This is what Alan, Hannah and Zoe did last weekend. Write answers for you, then use the information to write questions and short answers.

	Alan	Hannah and Zoe	You
play computer games	✗	✓	
go shopping	✓	✗	
play the piano	✗	✓	
cook a meal	✓	✗	
read a book	✓	✗	
do some homework	✗	✓	

Did Alan play computer games?
No, he didn't.
Did you do any homework at the weekend?
Yes, I did.

Past simple: *Wh-* questions

question word	did	subject	verb
Who	did	I/you/he/she/it/we/you/they	see?
Where			go?

2 Match the beginnings and the ends of the questions.
1 Where   a) like the museum?
2 What   b) did he get up?
3 Did she   c) did Olivia go?
4 What time   d) is your birthday?
5 How long   e) did you have for lunch?
6 When   f) did she need to do her homework?

3 Write past simple questions.
1 Why / give him / my comic ?
  Why did you give him my comic?
2 you / go out / last night ?
3 What / they / have for dinner ?
4 When / Jack / start school ?
5 Where / she / go on holiday ?
6 you / have / a good weekend ?

4 Match the answers to the questions in Exercise 3.
a) I don't know. He didn't tell me.
b) She went to Peru.
c) They had fish and chips.
d) Yes. I went to the cinema.
e) Yes, it was wonderful. We went skydiving.
f) Because it was interesting.

5 Write the questions for these answers.
1 I got up at 7 am.
  What time did you get up?
2 They arrived at school at 9 am.
3 We had cheese sandwiches and apple juice for lunch.
4 I came to school by bike.
5 She did her homework after school.
6 They played basketball yesterday evening.

6 Answer the questions for you.
1 What did you do at the weekend?
2 Where did you go for your last holiday?
3 What did you have for breakfast?
4 What did you get for your birthday last year?
5 When did you last go to the zoo?
6 What was your favourite toy when you were a baby?

Grammar reference

Unit 8

be going to: affirmative and negative

+	I	am ('m)	going to	have lunch. watch a film.
	He/She/It	is ('s)		
	We/You/They	are ('re)		
−	I	am not ('m not)		
	He/She/It	is not (isn't)		
	We/You/They	are not (aren't)		

- We use *be going to* to talk about future plans and intentions.
  She's going to take her camera on holiday but she isn't going to take her laptop.
- To form the *be going to* future, use *be + going to + infinitive*.
  We're going to have dinner in a restaurant, but we aren't going to stay late.

be going to: questions and short answers

?	(What)	Am	I	going to	win?
		Is	he/she/it		
		Are	we/you/they		
+	Yes,	I am.			
		he/she/it is.			
		we/you/they are.			
−	No,	I'm not.			
		he/she/it isn't.			
		we/you/they aren't.			

- We form *yes/no* questions with *be* before the subject.
  Is he going to tell us the answers?
- To form *Wh-* questions, put a question word before *be*.
  What are you going to wear to the party?

1 Write sentences using (*be*) *going to*.
 1 They / go shopping on Saturday.
   They're going to go shopping on Saturday.
 2 Andrew / phone me tonight.
 3 I / play my favourite song.
 4 You / watch a film on DVD.
 5 My mum / help me.
 6 We / ride our bikes.

2 Write the sentences in the negative.
 1 Josh is going to tidy his bedroom.
   Josh isn't going to tidy his bedroom.
 2 I'm going to study Maths.
 3 Rebecca's going to get up early tomorrow.
 4 Carl and Simon are going to wear shorts.
 5 We're going to take our MP3 players.
 6 You're going to buy a new mobile phone.

3 Write questions with (*be*) *going to*.
 1 What time / Lily / arrive?
   What time is Lily going to arrive?
 2 Where / they / get married?
 3 How long / you / be on holiday?
 4 Why / Aiden / buy a new camera?
 5 What / you / wear to the party?
 6 When / it / stop raining?

will/won't for future prediction

+	I/You/He/She/It/We/They	will	sing.
−	I/You/He/She/It/We/They	won't	
?	Will	I/you/he/she/it/we/they	sing?
+	Yes,	I/you/he/she/it/we/they	will.
−	No,	I/you/he/she/it/we/they	won't.

- We use *will* (*will not / won't*) + *infinitive* without *to* to talk about a future prediction.
  I'm sure I'll have a lovely time.
- To form *yes/no* questions, put *will* before the subject.
  Will it be cold in the mountains?
- To form *Wh-* questions, put a question word before *will*.
  What will you do on holiday?

4 Write sentences about your future using the prompts in the box and the future with *will/won't*.

> go to university   travel round the world
> get an interesting job   learn another language

I think I'll go to university, but I won't travel round the world first …

5 Write questions with *will* then answer them for you.
 1 When / your lesson finish?
 2 Who / you see after school?
 3 What / you watch on the TV this evening?
 4 What / you eat for supper tonight?

Vocabulary Bank

UNIT 1

🧠 Jog your memory!

Look at the picture. Cover the rest of the page. How many family and friends words can you remember?

Family and friends (page 11)

aunt	granddad	parents
best friend	granddaughter	sister
brother	grandma	son
classmates	grandparents	teammates
cousin	grandson	uncle
dad	husband	
daughter	mum	

1 Look at the words in the box. Find pairs of words.
uncle – aunt

2 Test your partner. Say one word in a pair. Your partner says the other word. Then swap.
A: *aunt*
B: *uncle*
A: *sister*
B: …

Describing People (page 14)

blue	good-looking	red
brown	green	short
curly	intelligent	spiky
dark	long	straight
fair	old	tall
funny	pretty	young

1 Look at the words in the box. Write sentences about your friends and family. Use *has / have got*.

2 Talk about the people you know.
My sister's name is Ana. She's got curly hair …

🔍 Explore adjectives with *un-* and *-ful* (pages 12 & 17)

Look at the words in the box. Write the words in the correct column.

| beauty | colour | lucky | usual | care | happy | use | wonder |

un-	-ful
	beautiful

Friends and family
mum/dad

Describing people
hair – brown, curly, spiky

📓 Study tip

Start a vocabulary notebook or a vocabulary box with cards. Keep a record of all your new words. Add the words on this page under the headings *Friends and family* and *Describing people*.

Vocabulary Bank 107

Vocabulary Bank

UNIT 2

🧠 Jog your memory!

Look at the pictures. Cover the rest of the page. How many daily routine expressions can you remember? For example, *have a shower*.

Think again

Daily Routines (page 21)

brush	a shower
do	breakfast
get	dressed
go	lunch
have	my teeth
	some exercise
	to bed
	to school
	up

1 Turn to page 21. Look at the words under the photos for two minutes.

2 Can you remember them all? Match the words in the box to make expressions.
go to bed

After school activities (page 24)

art classes	drama	music
chess	football	swimming
dance classes	karate	tennis

1 Look at the words in the box. Match the words to the correct verbs.

play	have	do	go
	art classes		

2 Put the activities in order from your favourite (1) to your least favourite (9). Compare with a partner.
1 music, 2 karate, …

🔍 Explore prepositions of time (page 22)

December	lunchtime	July	8 o'clock
the afternoon	the weekend	night	Mondays

1 Look at the words in the box. Match them to the correct time phrases.

in	at	on

2 Work with a partner. Tell your partner what you usually do at each of these times.
In July my family go on holiday to the beach.

🔍 Explore expressions with *have* 1 (page 27)

13 years old	a shower	a bath	cold
a cold	breakfast	a drink	a rest
hungry	a snack	dinner	lunch

1 Look at the words in the box. Which *three* words do *not* go with *have*?

2 Write true and false sentences for you. Use phrases with *have*. Work with a partner. Guess which sentences are true and false.
I have a bath every Sunday.

I have supper at 7.30.
We have a break every day at 11.30.

📅 Study tip

Always write examples of words that go together in your vocabulary notebook. This will help you not to make mistakes when you use the word in your speaking and writing.

Vocabulary Bank

UNIT 3

🧠 Jog your memory!

Look at the pictures. Cover the rest of the page. How many places in a school can you remember?

Think again

Places in school (page 33)

canteen	library	science lab
classroom	main hall	sports hall
IT room	playing field	

1 Work with a partner. Look at the words in the box. Choose a room. Don't tell your partner. Say three things you can find in the room. Can your partner guess which room it is?

A: *You find books, computers and pens in this room.*
B: *Is it the IT room?*
A: *Yes, it is!*

School subjects (page 36)

English	History	Music
French	ICT	PE
Geography	Maths	Science

1 Look at the words in the box. What is your perfect school day? Complete the timechart.

8.30–9.45	9.45–11	11–11.15	11.15–12.15
PE			

12.15–1.15	1.15–2.15	2.15–2.30	2.30–3

🔍 Explore nouns and verbs (page 34)

~~exercise~~	practise	study	training
practice	studies	train	

1 Complete the chart with words from the list.

verb	noun
exercise	

2 Can you add three more nouns and two more verbs to the chart?

🔍 Explore adjectives (page 39)

boring	great	terrible
brilliant	interesting	
fast	slow	

1 Look again at page 34. Can you find three more adjectives in the Kung-Fu text?

2 Think of a word for each adjective.
boring – shopping

swim (verb/noun)

📓 Study tip

Write the part of speech next to new words in your vocabulary notebook. It helps you to use them correctly in your work.

Vocabulary Bank 109

Vocabulary Bank

UNIT 4

🧠 Jog your memory!

Look at the picture. Cover the rest of the page. How many types of food and meals can you remember?

Food (page 43)

apples	carrot	meat
banana	cheese	milk
beans	chicken	pasta
bread	eggs	pizza
butter	fish	rice

1. Look at the words in the box. Write the words in order of how often you eat or drink them from most often to least often.

2. Compare your list with your partner.
   I eat bananas more often than Harry. He eats carrots more often than me!

3. Can you add three more food words to the list?

🔍 Explore expressions with *have* 2
(page 44)

breakfast	a snack	a problem
lunch	a party	a look
dinner	fun	a good time

1. Look at the words in the box. Write five sentences. Use *have* and five of the words in the box.
   I always have a good time when I go out with my friends.

2. Swap your sentences with your partner. Check that your partner's sentences are correct.

Meals and courses (page 46)

breakfast	lunch	snack
dessert	main course	starter
dinner		

1. What is your favourite meal for each course? Talk to your partner about your lists.
   My favourite breakfast is eggs and coffee.

2. Do you eat snacks? What type of snacks do you eat?

3. Plan a menu. Write down food for the starter, main course and dessert.
   Starter: pasta with …

🔍 Explore international words (page 49)

burger	pizza	sushi	taco

1. Look at the words in the box. Which country are they from?

2. Write down five more international words.

📓 Study tip

Sort words in your vocabulary notebook by topic. You can also record them in a mind map.

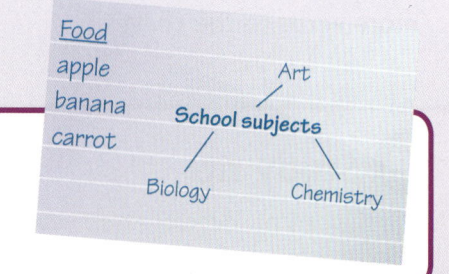

Vocabulary Bank

UNIT 5

Jog your memory!

Look at the pictures. Cover the rest of the page. How many animals can you find in one minute?

Animals (page 55)

bird	giraffe	shark
cat	gorilla	sheep
cow	horse	spider
dog	monkey	tiger
elephant	polar bear	zebra
fish		

1 Look at the words in the box. Write the animals in the correct column.

land	air	sea
cat		

2 Cover the chart and test your partner.
A: Dog.
B: Land.
A: Correct! Your turn!

3 Which of the animals are fast, slow, dangerous or intelligent?

Action verbs (page 58)

| fight | hide | jump | swing |
| fly | hunt | swim | |

1 Look at the words in the box. Write sentences about animals for each verb.
My cat fights with my dog.

2 Close your books. Work with a partner. Say a sentence. Your partner guesses the animal.
A: It swims in the sea.
B: A fish?
A: No, a shark.

Explore adverbs of movement (page 56)

| backwards | left | round | forwards |
| down | right | up | |

| go | sit | stand | turn |

1 Look at the words in the boxes. Use words from each box to write instructions.
1 *Stand up.* 2 *Turn left.*

2 Work with a partner. Read your instructions. Your partner does the actions. Then swap.

Explore the suffix -er (page 61)

clean	have	study	want
dance	paint	teach	write
drive	sing		

1 Look at the words in the box. Add -er to seven of the verbs to make words to describe what people do.

2 Do you know anyone who does these jobs? Would you like to do any of these jobs? Talk with your partner.

Jump (verb)
Kangaroos jump higher than horses!

Study tip

Write an example sentence next to the new words in your vocabulary book. This will remind you how to use the new words and it will help you to remember them.

Vocabulary Bank

UNIT 6

Jog your memory!

Look at the pictures. Cover the rest of the page. How many places can you remember?

Places in a town 1 (page 65)

bowling alley	museum	sports centre
cinema	shopping centre	sports stadium
market	skate park	

Look at the words in the box. Where can you …
- buy food?
- watch something?
- do some exercise?
- learn something?
- buy a present for a friend?

Places in a town 2 (page 68)

bus station	ferry port	station
bus stop	market	tram stop
car park		

1. Look at the words in the box. Which places are there in your town?

2. Work with a partner. Choose one of the places, but don't tell your partner. Describe where it is and what you do there. Your partner guesses the place. Then swap.

Explore extreme adjectives (page 66)

ancient   boiling   great   beautiful   enormous   terrified

1. Look at the extreme adjectives in the box. Match them with the meanings in the chart. Can you add any others?

Meaning	Extreme adjectives
very old	
very big	
very hot	
very scared	
very pretty	
very good	

2. Write a sentence for each adjective.
   The church in my town. (ancient)

3. Work with a partner. Say your sentences. Your partner guesses the adjective.

Explore collocations (page 71)

go by   go on   take the

bike   bus   foot   taxi   train   tram

1. Look at the words in boxes. How many collocations can you make?
   go by bike, take the bus

2. Work with a partner. Tell your partner about a very long journey.
   First I took a taxi to the station, then I took the train to …

Study tip

Draw pictures next to words in your vocabulary book to help you remember the meaning. Some people prefer pictures to help them remember new words. Some people prefer definitions. Which do you prefer?

Vocabulary Bank

UNIT 7

🧠 Jog your memory!

Look at the pictures. Cover the rest of the page. How many sports can you name?

Sport (page 77)

baseball	judo	surfing
basketball	skateboarding	volleyball
bowling	skiing	windsurfing
cycling	snowboarding	

1. Look at the words in the box. Match the sports with the correct verbs.

   go   play   do   *go bowling*

2. Look back at page 77 and check your answers.

3. Talk to your partner. Which sports do you enjoy watching? Which are dangerous?

4. Work with a partner. Test him/her. Close your books. Say a sport. Your partner says the correct verb, *play*, *do* or *go*.

🔍 Explore adverbs (page 78)

general	surprising	traditional	typical	usual

1. Look at the adjectives in the box. Make them into adverbs. Use a dictionary and the text on page 78, to help you.
   general – generally

2. Choose four of the words. Write four sentences using the words.

Clothes (page 80)

boots	jacket	skirt	tracksuit
cap	jeans	socks	trousers
hoodie	shorts	sweatshirt	T-shirt

1. Look at the words in the box. Which clothes do you usually wear …
   - to do sport?
   - when it's hot?
   - when it's cold?
   - to go shopping?

2. Work with a partner. Look at the words for one minute. Close your books. How many clothes words can you write in two minutes? Open your book and check your answers together. Is your spelling correct?

🔍 Explore irregular plurals (page 83)

child	man	reindeer	tooth
fish	mouse	sheep	woman

1. Look at the plural words on page 83 for 30 seconds. Close your books. How many of the words can you write down in one minute?

2. Look at the words in the box. What are the plural forms? Look in a dictionary to check your answers.

📇 Study tip

Make vocabulary flashcards to help you revise your vocabulary. Write a definition or draw a picture, whatever is best for you.

Vocabulary Bank   113

Vocabulary Bank

UNIT 8

🧠 Jog your memory!

Look at the pictures. Cover the rest of the page. How many weather words can you remember?

Weather and seasons (page 87)

Seasons			
autumn	spring	summer	winter

Weather adjectives			
cloudy	icy	snowy	sunny
foggy	rainy	stormy	windy

1. Look at the words in the boxes. What's the weather like in your country?
   In spring in my country, it's …

2. Work with a partner. Take turns to close your books and test your spelling. Which word has a silent consonant?

3. The weather words are all adjectives. Write the noun for each word.
   sunny – sun

Landscapes (page 90)

beach	hill	mountains
desert	jungle	river
forest	lake	sea

1. Look at the words in the box. What types of landscape do you have in your country?

2. Draw a landscape. Include at least five of the words.

3. Describe your picture to your partner. He/She listens and draws it. Check your partner's picture. Is it the same as yours?

🔍 Explore collocations (page 88)

1. Look at the chart. Add the following words to the correct column. Sometimes a word can go in more than one column.

a break	a train	time
at home	in a bus	photos

Stay	spend	take
in a hostel	a day	a bike
in a hotel	a week	a camera
in a cabin		
in a treehouse		

2. Work with a partner. A, say a word from the box. B, guess which verb you use it with.
   A: *A camera.*   B: *Take.*

🔍 Explore adjectives (page 93)

1. Can you think of two nouns for each of the adjectives below?

popular	person
perfect	day
special	
amazing	
luxury	
excellent	

2. Work with a partner. Read your lists of nouns. Your partner guesses which adjective describes them.

📖 Study tip

Study with a friend – test yourself and each other. Use your vocabulary notebook or cards.

1 CLIL

Maths Fractions

1 Read the definition. Match the pictures with the fractions.

A fraction is part of a whole or complete number.

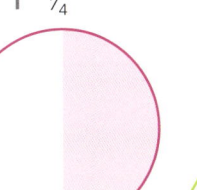

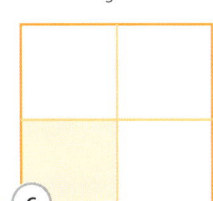

1 ¼   2 ½   3 ⅓

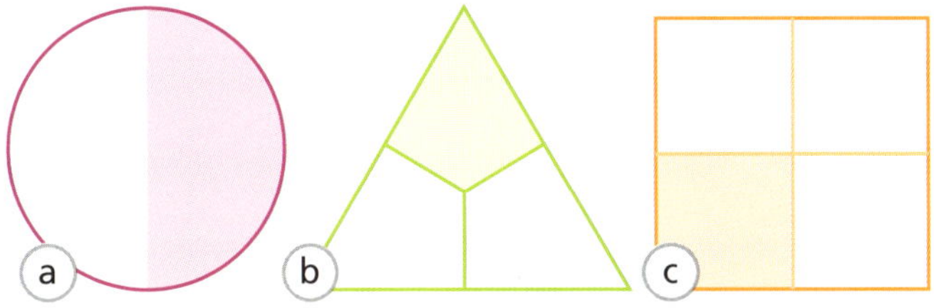

a   b   c

2 Match the fractions with their names.

1 c

1 ½   a) a third
2 ¼   b) a seventh
3 ⅓   c) a half
4 ⅙   d) a fifth
5 ⅕   e) a sixth
6 ⅐   f) an eighth
7 ⅛   g) three quarters
8 ¾   h) a quarter

3 🔊 1.42 Listen, check and repeat.

4 Read the text and look at the pictures. Which number (1 or 8) is the numerator? Which is the denominator?

Ana has got a cake. She eats 1/8.

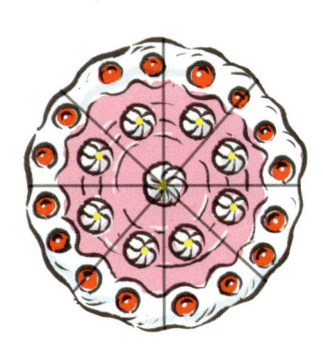

The denominator is the total number of equal parts.
The numerator is the number of parts Ana eats.

5 Read the quiz. Choose the correct options.

Ben and John have got a pizza. It's got eight pieces.

1 Ben eats two pieces. He eats …
   a ¼   b ½   c ¾   of the pizza.

2 John eats four pieces. He eats …
   a ¼   b ½   c ¾   of the pizza.

3 They don't eat …
   a ¼   b ½   c ⅛   of the pizza.

Your turn

6 Work with a partner. Write a quiz like the one in Exercise 5. Show your quiz to the class. Think about …
- another type of food.
- the denominator.
- the numerator that people eat each time.

Find out about Australia in fractions.

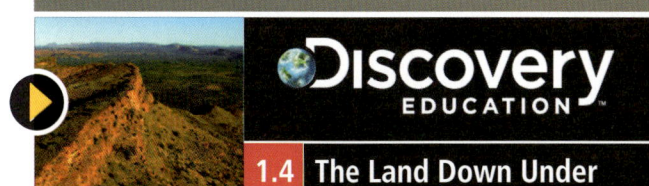

1.4 The Land Down Under

Discovery EDUCATION

115

2 CLIL

Science The Earth's movements

1 Work with a partner. Look at the picture and do the quiz.

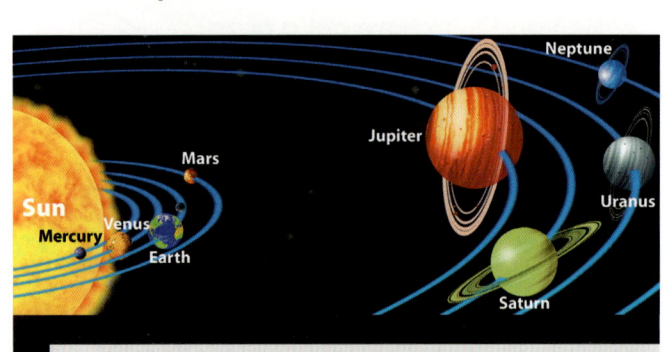

World of wonder

1 The Earth is a …
   a) star.   b) planet.   c) solar system.

2 How many planets revolve around the Sun?
   a) seven   b) eight   c) nine

3 The Sun is a …
   a) star.   b) planet.   c) solar system.

4 The Earth revolves around the Sun at …
   a) 52,000 km per hour.
   b) 108,000 km per hour.
   c) 143,000 km per hour.

5 The Earth revolves around the Sun in …
   a) 24 hours.   b) 365.25 days.   c) 7 days.

6 The Earth has got a satellite. It's called …
   a) the Moon.   b) the Sun.   c) Jupiter.

7 The Moon revolves around the Earth. It takes …
   a) 24 hours.   b) 7 days.   c) 27 days.

2 🔊 1.43 Listen and check your answers.

3 🔊 1.44 Read the text. Then match the sentence halves below.

DAY AND NIGHT

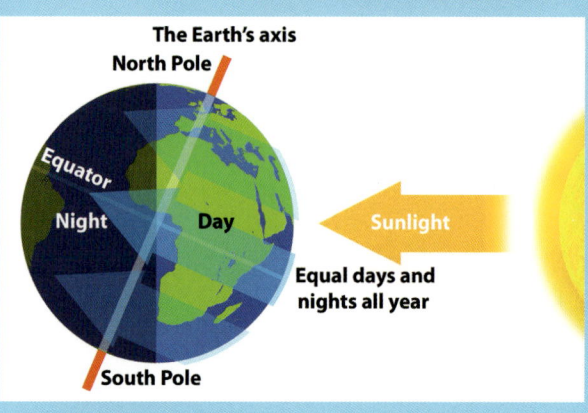

The Earth revolves around the Sun and it also rotates on its axis. Imagine a line from the North Pole to the South Pole; that's the Earth's axis. The Earth makes one complete rotation every 24 hours. 24 hours is one complete day and one complete night. When a part of the Earth faces the Sun, it's day. When a part of the Earth faces away from the Sun, it's night.

1 The Earth's axis is a line …
2 The Earth rotates on its axis …
3 It's day when part of the Earth …
4 It's night when part of the Earth …

a) faces away from the Sun.
b) faces the Sun.
c) every 24 hours.
d) from the North Pole to the South Pole.

Your turn

4 Choose a planet. Use the Internet, books or magazines to find out information about it. Think about …
- distance from the Sun.
- number of moons.
- time of rotation around the Sun in days.
- duration of a day.

Find out about the planet Mars.

Discovery EDUCATION
2.4 Mars

3 CLIL

Design and Technology Drawing tools

1 🔊 **1.45** Look at the picture. Match the drawing tools with the words in the box. Then listen and check.

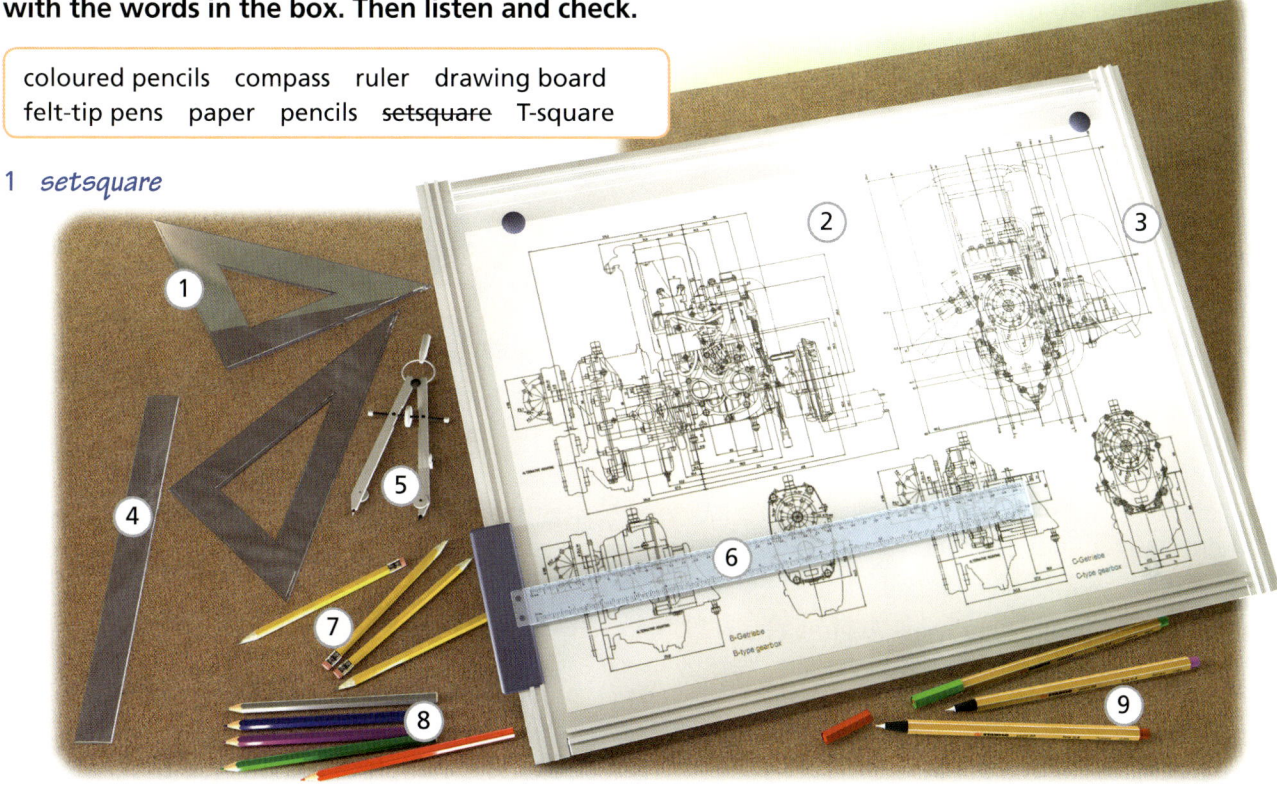

> coloured pencils   compass   ruler   drawing board
> felt-tip pens   paper   pencils   ~~setsquare~~   T-square

1 *setsquare*

2 Complete the table about the drawing tools with the words in the box.

> angles   circles   colour   straight
> ~~paper~~   parallel

1 *paper*

drawing board	We put ¹ … on this.
t-square	We draw ² … lines with this.
setsquare	We draw ³ … of 90°, 45°, 30° and 60° with these.
compass	We draw ⁴ … and curved lines with these.
ruler	We draw ⁵ … lines and calculate the length of a line with this.
felt-tip pens	We ⁶ … our design with these.

3 🔊 **1.46** Listen to the conversation and check your answers.

4 Which drawing tools in Exercise 1 do you use …
- in Maths?
- in Art?
- in both?

5 Look at the shapes. Copy them. What drawing tools do you need?

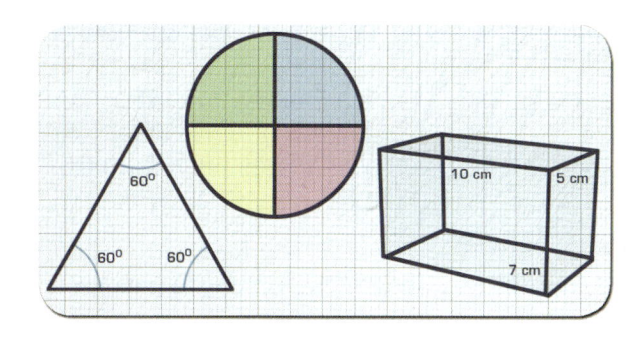

Your turn

6 Work with a partner. Describe the drawing tools in Exercise 1. Your partner guesses what they are.

> We draw angles with these.   A set square?

Find out about Leonardo da Vinci's designs for a cart.

Discovery EDUCATION

3.4 Da Vinci's design

117

4 CLIL

Geography Climate and Food

1. Look at the pictures. Can you name the food items? Where do they grow? What climate do they need to grow? Think about rainfall and temperature.

2. 🔊 **1.47** Listen, check and repeat the food words.

3. 🔊 **1.48** Read the text. Complete the missing information in the map's key.

- In a **polar climate** it's always cold. The temperature never goes above 10 °C. It's very difficult to grow food here because the winters are very long and dark. People usually eat a lot of meat and fish but not much fresh fruit or vegetables.

- Turkey, California and southwest Australia have a **Mediterranean climate**. It's hot in the summer and rainy in the winter. They use irrigation systems to grow crops like oranges and figs. Olive trees grow well in the Mediterranean climate because they don't need much water. The Mediterranean diet includes a lot of vegetables and not much fat.

- Saudi Arabia and Egypt have a **desert climate**. Daytime temperatures are high all year but it can be cold at night. It doesn't rain very often and not many plants grow in these areas. Date palms grow near oases. Dates are nutritious and they are an important part of the desert nomads' diet.

- Malaysia and Congo have a **tropical climate**, with high temperatures and a lot of rain all year round. Plants grow easily in these conditions. Rice, bananas and sugar cane grow on large farms or *plantations*. In these countries, people eat a lot of rice.

4. 🔊 **1.48** Read the text again and check your answers to Exercise 1.

Map key:
- Polar climate
- Temperate climate
- _____
- Mediterranean
- Mountains

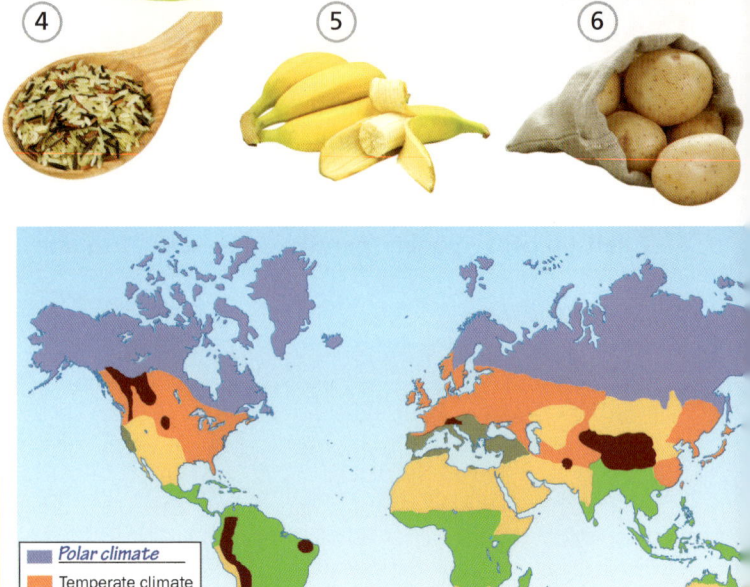

Weather: the day-to-day changes in temperature, rain and wind.

Climate: the typical weather in a local area.

5. Copy and complete the table with information from the text.

	Country	Climate	Crops	Diet
Polar climate			none	meat, fish
Mediterranean climate				
Desert climate				
Tropical climate				

Your turn

6. Work with a partner. Choose four different types of food. Find out …
   - what climate they need to grow.
   - if they grow in more than one climate.
   - if the farmers use special methods to cultivate them.

Find out about rice growing in China.

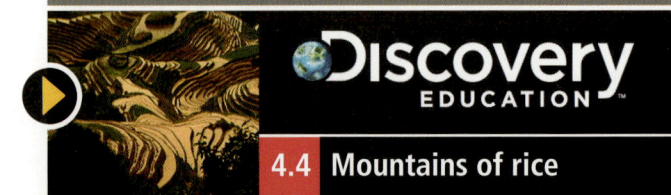

Discovery EDUCATION

4.4 Mountains of rice

5 CLIL

Science Vertebrates

1 Look at the pictures in the text. What animals can you see?

2 🔊 2.39 Read the text. Think of another example for each animal group.
bird: flamingo

3 🔊 2.39 Read the text again. Write the correct vertebrate group(s) for each statement.
1. They can usually fly. *birds*
2. Their young are born from eggs.
3. Their young form inside their bodies.
4. They haven't got lungs.
5. They haven't got arms or legs.
6. They've got skin, fur or feathers.
7. They don't live on land.
8. They can live in water and on land.

Your turn

4 Work with a partner. Student A describes an animal, and Student B guesses the animal. Use the vocabulary in Exercise 2.

Animals with BACKBONES

1 Birds
Birds have got two legs, two wings and feathers on their bodies. Most birds can fly, but some birds, like penguins, can't. Baby chicks are born or 'hatch' from eggs.

2 Fish
All fish live in water and use gills to breathe. Fish haven't got arms or legs, but they have got fins for swimming. They've got scales on their bodies. All baby fish are born from eggs.

3 Mammals
Most mammals have got hair, skin or fur on their bodies. Baby mammals are born from their mothers and drink milk. Some mammals live in water but they breathe with lungs out of the water.

4 Reptiles
All reptiles, except snakes, have got four legs. They've also got scales, and some, like chameleons, can change colour. Baby reptiles are born from eggs.

5 Amphibians
Baby frogs, or tadpoles, are born in water from eggs and breathe with gills. Adult amphibians have got lungs and they can live on land or in water. They've got smooth skin.

Find out about chameleons and their habitat.

5.4 Chameleons

6 CLIL

Art Images and communication

1 Work with a partner. Look at the sentences and communicate the information.
1. 'I'm OK!' (Use your hands.)
2. 'That's really funny!' (Use a sound.)
3. 'Stop!' (Draw an image.)

2 🔊 2.40 Read the text. Match the images (1–3) with their communicative purpose (A–C).

IMAGES AROUND US

We often communicate with images. Images send us a message. Some images inform us, some tell us to do something, and others simply entertain us. Let's look at the images around us in our towns and cities.

A INFORMATIVE IMAGES
A lot of images in towns and cities inform us about things, for example maps, road signs, shop logos and posters. These images are usually simple and give us very clear messages.

B PERSUASIVE IMAGES
These images tell us to do something. You can see lots of these images in advertisements in the street. They usually want to sell us something, for example a drink, clothes or a ticket to the cinema.

C RECREATIONAL IMAGES
These images entertain us, for example images from films, comics or even street art and graffiti. These images attract our attention because they are beautiful, strange or surprising. They make the town or city more interesting or attractive.

3 🔊 2.41 Listen to the conversation. Which types of images in the box do Jessica and Simon take photos of?

> logo   map   pictogram   poster   sign
> graffiti   diagram

Your turn

4 Work with a partner. Look at images in your school. What is their communicative purpose? Make a list.

Find out about ancient and modern art in Mexico.

Discovery EDUCATION

6.4 Big art

7 CLIL

PE Outdoor sports and activities

1 Look at the pictures. Where do we do these sports and activities? Copy and complete the table.

On land	In the air	On water
climbing		

climbing • windsurfing • bungee jumping • horse riding • paragliding • canoeing

2 🔊 **2.42** Read the text. Check your ideas in Exercise 1.

Outdoor sports and activities

We often do sports and activities at a gym or a sports centre, but sometimes we do them outdoors, in a natural environment. Outdoor sports and activities are sometimes competitive. This means that we do them in a race or a competition because we want to win a prize. Recreational means that we do them because they are fun.

We usually do outdoor sports and activities in three different places: on land, in the air or in the water. Horse riding, mountain biking and climbing are land activities. We often go climbing on mountains or large rocks. Bungee jumping, parachuting and paragliding are air activities. We jump from a high place like a bridge when we do bungee jumping. Canoeing, waterskiing and windsurfing are water activities. We go canoeing in rivers and waterskiing and windsurfing in the sea.

3 Check the meaning of the words in the box.

helmet   goggles   gloves   wetsuit
waterproof clothes   life jacket

4 🔊 **2.43** Listen and write the sports for each piece of equipment in Exercise 3.

helmet: mountain biking, canoeing, climbing

Your turn

5 Work with a partner. Choose an outdoor sport or activity. Find out information about it and make a poster. Use the ideas below.
- Is it a land, air or water activity?
- Where can you do it in your country?
- What special clothes or protection do you need?
- Is it a competitive or recreational activity or both?

Find out about extreme fishing in the USA.

Discovery EDUCATION

7.4 Extreme fishing

8 CLIL

Maths Frequency tables and bar charts

1. Work with a partner. Look at the picture of class 1B's favourite sports and read the text. Answer the questions.

   - 'Data total' is the total amount of information in a mathematical study.
   - 'Frequency' is how often something appears in mathematical data.

   1. What is the data total for Class 1B's favourite sports?
   2. What is the frequency of tennis?

2. Look at the picture in Exercise 1 again. What is the frequency of each sport? Copy and complete the table.

	Number of students
football	9
cycling	
rollerblading	
basketball	
tennis	2
swimming	
total	

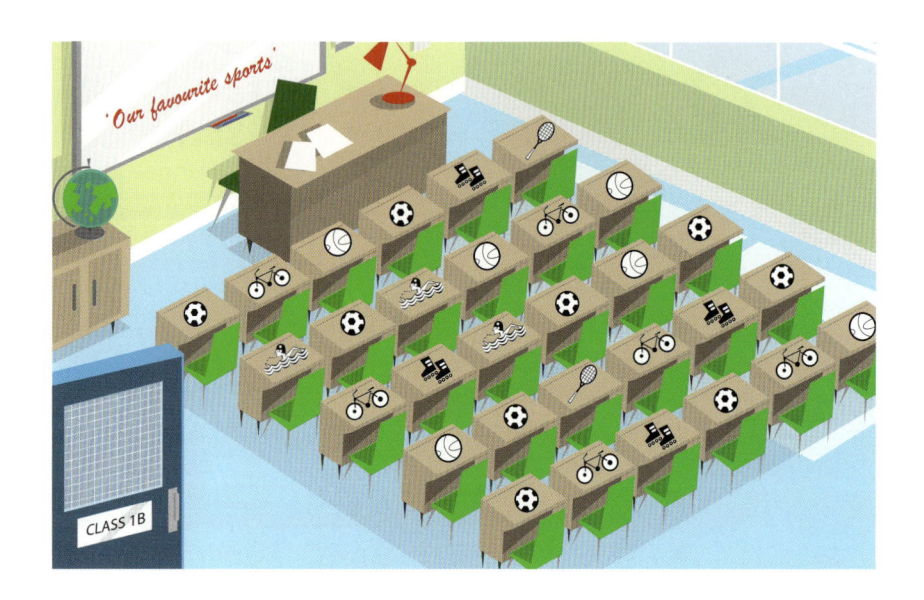

3. Look at the information from Exercise 2 in a bar chart. Answer the questions.
   1. Which data is wrong?
   2. Which axis (X or Y) is a horizontal line? Which is a vertical line?

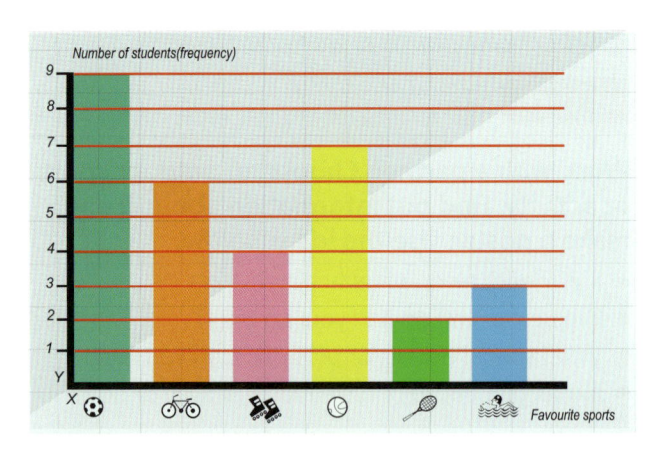

Your turn

4. Work with a partner. Ask students in your class where they are going to spend their summer holidays. Then make a frequency table and a bar chart with the information. Use these ideas.
   - the beach
   - the mountains
   - a city
   - visit family or friends

Find out about holiday activities in Australia in the summer.

Discovery EDUCATION

8.4 Holiday in Australia

Project 1

A class survey

Class Survey: *favourite gadget*

1 What's your favourite gadget?
2 Who's it from?
3 When do you use it?
4 Where do you use it?

(Pie chart categories: computer, MP3 player, digital camera, games console, mobile phone)

Look

1 Look at the class survey and the pie chart. Which 'gadget' is the most popular?

2 Answer the questions in the survey for you.

Prepare

3 Work in groups of three or four. Choose one of the topics for a class survey.
- after school activities
- daily routines
- family members
- languages

4 Write questions about the topic in Exercise 3. Use the question words below.

What … ?   Where … ?   Who … ?
When … ?   Which … ?   How many … ?

5 Ask your classmates the questions in your survey.

Present

6 Draw a pie chart like the one in Exercise 1 to show your results. Present your results to the rest of the class.

Project 2

A wildlife poster

Look

1 Read the text. Match the descriptions with the photos.

1 They're pink and they've got very long legs. They live in Africa, South America and parts of Asia — usually near water. They don't usually swim but they can fly. They're very sociable animals and they live in big groups. They eat shrimps and plankton in the water.

2 They're usually black, orange and white. They've got big teeth and are very strong and fast. They live in India, Russia and China. They're very territorial and can swim very well. They're carnivores and they eat other animals like buffalo and deer. They're an 'endangered species' — there are only about 3,000 left in the world!

3 They've got six legs and are usually brown. They live together in big colonies. They live all over the world except in Antarctica. There are usually thousands in each colony. There are soldiers, workers and a queen. They can carry very heavy things and can find their colony from long distances. They eat plants, fruit, fungus and insects.

Prepare

2 Work in groups of three. Choose three animals from your country. Use the Internet, books or magazines to find information about them. Think about …
- physical appearance.
- habitat.
- abilities/behaviour.
- food/diet.

3 Find photos of the animals in Exercise 2. Make a poster with the photos and the information about each animal. Put the photos in a different order from the information.

Present

4 Present your poster to the rest of the class in your group. Can they guess which information is about each animal?

Project 3

A tourist information poster

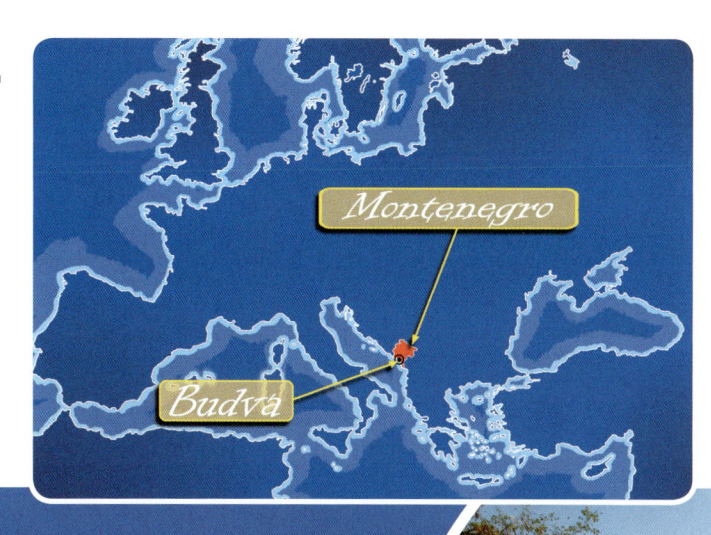

Look

1 Read the information about Budva. Answer the questions.
   1 Where is Budva?
   2 What's its history?
   3 What can you see/do there?
   4 What's the weather like?
   5 How do you get there?

BUDVA

Where is it?
Budva is a city on the Adriatic Coast in Montenegro in south-eastern Europe. Not many people know it but it's very popular with millionaires! Budva has a long history – it's 3,500 years old. It was a small fishing village 50 years ago, but now rich people from Italy, Austria and Russia have houses in the town.

A historical town
It's very old and beautiful. There's an Old Town. Some people think this part of Budva was an island in the past. Now it's part of the town. The Venetians (people from Venice) ruled the town from 1420 to 1797 and they built walls to defend the town from their enemies. These walls are now popular with tourists.

Music
It's also a great place for music and concerts. A lot of famous musicians go to play concerts there – *the Rolling Stones* played in 2007. 35,000 people came to see them and the town has only got 16,000 residents! Madonna and David Guetta also played in Budva.

Relax!
There are lots of local beaches. Mogren Beach is very popular and is only 500 metres from the Old Town. The town's got a Mediterranean climate so it's usually warm and sunny.

How to get there
You can fly to Tivat or Podgorica airport or come by car along the Adriatic Highway.

Prepare

2 Work in groups of three or four. Choose a town or city. Use the Internet, books or magazines to find information about it. Use the questions in Exercise 1 to help you.

3 Find photos of the town or city. Make a poster with the photos and the information in Exercise 2.

Present

4 Present your poster to the rest of the class in your group. Which town would the class most like to visit?

Irregular verbs

infinitive	past simple	past participle
be	was/were	been
become	became	become
begin	began	begun
break	broke	broken
build	built	built
buy	bought	bought
catch	caught	caught
choose	chose	chosen
come	came	come
do	did	done
drink	drank	drunk
drive	drove	driven
eat	ate	eaten
fall	fell	fallen
feed	fed	fed
feel	felt	felt
find	found	found
fly	flew	flown
get	got	got
give	gave	given
go	went	gone
have	had	had
hear	heard	heard
keep	kept	kept
know	knew	known
learn	learnt/learned	learnt/learned
leave	left	left
lose	lost	lost
make	made	made
meet	met	met
pay	paid	paid
put	put	put
read	read	read
run	ran	run
say	said	said
see	saw	seen
send	sent	sent
sit	sat	sat
sleep	slept	slept
speak	spoke	spoken
spend	spent	spent
swim	swam	swum
take	took	taken
teach	taught	taught
tell	told	told
think	thought	thought
wear	wore	worn
win	won	won
write	wrote	written

Phonemic script

consonants

/p/	pencil
/b/	bag
/t/	town
/d/	day
/tʃ/	cheese
/dʒ/	juice
/k/	cake
/g/	get
/f/	food
/v/	very
/θ/	Thursday
/ð/	that
/s/	speak
/z/	zebra
/ʃ/	shoe
/ʒ/	usually
/m/	mum
/n/	name
/ŋ/	sing
/h/	house
/l/	like
/r/	red
/w/	water
/j/	you

vowels

/iː/	see
/ɪ/	sit
/ʊ/	book
/uː/	zoo
/e/	pen
/ə/	teacher
/ɜː/	bird
/ɔː/	boring
/æ/	that
/ʌ/	run
/ɑː/	car
/ɒ/	lost

diphthongs

/eɪ/	say
/ɪə/	hear
/ʊə/	pure
/ɔɪ/	enjoy
/əʊ/	know
/eə/	chair
/aɪ/	buy
/aʊ/	now

Thanks and acknowledgements

The authors and publishers would like to thank all the teachers and consultants who have contributed to the development of this course, in particular:

Argentina: Fernando Armesto; Natalia Bitar; Verónica Borrás; Leonor Corradi ; Paz Moltrasio; Diana Ogando; Brazil: Dalmo Carvalho; Roberto Costa; Sônia M. B. Leites; Gloria Paz; Litany Pires Ribeiro; Christina Riego; Renata Condi de Souza; Elizabeth White; Chile: Magdalena Aldunate; M. Cristina Darraidou Diaz; Valentina Donoso; Ana María Páez Jofrré; Ricardo Contreras Marambio; Claudia Ottone; Maria Elena Ramirez; Jacqueline Rondon; Alicia Paez Ubilla; Colombia: Luz Amparo Bautista; Sonia Ruiz Hernández; Sandra Jara; Fabian Jimenez; Bibiana Andrea Piñeros Merizalde; Lucero Amparo Bernal Nieto; Olga Olarte; Bibiana Piñeros; Emelis Rambut; Sonia Ruíz; Poland: Anna Bylicka; Russia: Natalya Melchenkova; Irina Polyakova; Svetlana Suchkova; Irina Vayserberg; Turkey: Ali Bilgin; Angela Çakır; Shirley Nuttal; Cinla Sezgin; Mujgan Yesiloglu

The publishers are grateful to the following for permission to reproduce copyright photographs and material:
Cover: Alamy/©Hakbong Kwon; p. 6: (1) Shutterstock Images/artjazz; p. 6: (2) Alamy/©Nikreates; p. 8: (2) Shutterstock Images/Andrea Izzotti: p. 8: (1) Alamy/© London Entertainment: p. 8: (4) Shutterstock Images/Evlakhov Valeriy: p. 8: (5) Alamy/©FocusJapan; p. 9: (TR) Alamy/©Glowimages RM; p. 9: (BR) Shutterstock Images/Tyler Olson; p. 10: (B/G) Shutterstock Images/Cora Mueller; p. 11: (BL) Shutterstock Images/Max Topchii: p. 11: (TL) Shutterstock Images/AlenD: p. 11: (TCL) Shutterstock Images/Shaun Jeffers: p. 11: (TR) Shutterstock Images/Igor Borodin: p. 11: (CL) Shutterstock Images/Dmitry Morgan: p. 11: (CL) Shutterstock Images/Olga Rosi; p. 12: (T) Photo Kevin Farmer / APN; p. 13: (TL) Photo Kevin Farmer / APN; p. 13: (TL) Shutterstock Images/v.s.anandhakrishna; p. 15: (b) Shutterstock Images/Fisher Photostudio; p. 16: (B) Alamy/©PhotoAlto sas; p. 16: (TR) Alamy/©RIA Novosti; p. 16: (CR) Alamy/©ARCTIC IMAGES; p. 17: (B/G) ©India Picture/Corbis; p. 18: (C) Shutterstock Images/Blend Images; p. 18: (CL) SuperStock/RubberBall; p. 18: (CRT) Shutterstock Images/CREATISTA; p. 18: (CRB) Alamy/©Radius Images; p. 18: (BRT) Shutterstock Images/Photosindiacom, LLC; p. 18: (BR) Alamy/©Young-Wolff Photography; p. 18: (TL) Shutterstock Images/Rob Stark; p. 19: (TR) Alamy/©RubberBall; p. 20: (B/G) Corbis/©Ned Frisk; p. 21: (a) Alamy/©amana images inc.; p. 21: (2) Alamy/©ableimages; p. 21: (3) Alamy/©Juice Images; p. 21: (d) Alamy/©Stuwdamdorp; p. 21: (e) Alamy/©vario images GmbH & Co.KG; p. 21: (f) Alamy/©Juice Images; p. 21: (g) Alamy/©Tetra Images; p. 21: (h) Alamy/©Blend Images; p. 21: (i) Alamy/©Stockbroker; p. 21: (j) Alamy/©Megapress; p. 21: (C) Thinkstock/Medioimages/Photodisc; p. 22: (CR) Shutterstock Images/Tracy Whiteside; p. 22: (BR) Shutterstock Images/Tracy Whiteside; p. 22: (BR) Alamy/©Megapress; p. 22: (TR): p. 22: (C) Shutterstock Images/BestPhotoStudio; p. 23: (B) Shutterstock Images/Jorg Hackemann; p. 24: (1) Shutterstock Images/Rob Marmion; p. 24: (2) Shutterstock Images/Mike Flippo; p. 24: (3) Shutterstock Images/dean bertoncelj; p. 24: (4) Shutterstock Images/Zhukov Oleg; p. 24: (5) Shutterstock Images/Be Good; p. 24: (6) Shutterstock Images/Anna Jurkovska; p. 24: (7) Shutterstock Images/Photosani; p. 24: (8) Shutterstock Images/Andrey Yurlov; p. 24: (9) Alamy/©Design Pics Inc; p. 26: (T) Shutterstock Images/LU JINRONG; p. 27: (TL) Alamy/©dbimages: p. 27: (B) Shutterstock Images/De Jongh Photography; p. 27: (R) Getty Images/ALEAIMAGE; p. 28: (TL) Alamy/©Daily Mail/Rex: p. 28: (CL) Shutterstock Images/Dmitry Kalinovsky; p. 29: (TR) Shutterstock Images/Max Topchii; p. 32: (B/G) Alamy/©paul kennedy; p. 34: (C) Alamy/©F. Jack Jackson; p. 35: (CL) Getty Images/blackwaterimages; p. 35: (CR) Getty Images/Vetta; p. 35: (C) Getty Images/blackwaterimages: p. 35: (R) Getty Images/Vetta; p. 36: (CR) Alamy/©Yuri Arcurs; p. 36: (C) Alamy/©Janine Wiedel Photolibrary; p. 36: (BL) Alamy/©Blend Images; p. 36: (C) Alamy/©Elvele Images Ltd; p. 36: (TR) Alamy/©nick baylis: p. 36: (B/G) Alamy/©Kari Marttila; p. 37: (TR) Getty Images/Blend Images: p. 37: (CR) Getty Images/Glowimages: p. 37: (BR) Getty Images/Ronald Martinez; p. 38: (B/G) Getty Images/Gallo Images ROOTS Collection: p. 38: (TR) Corbis/©David Turnley; pg. 39: (B/G) Getty Images/Turnervisual; p. 39: (TR) Getty Images/iconeer; p. 39: (CR) Getty Images/Image Source; p. 40: (CL) Getty Images/David Burch; p. 40: (BC) Getty Images/Skip Odonnell; p. 40: (BR) Getty Images/Fotosearch; p. 40: (TL) Alamy/©moodboard; p. 41: (TC) Getty Images/iconeer; p. 41: (TR) Alamy/©Juice Images; p. 42: (B/G) Shutterstock Images/Gyorgy Barna; p. 43: (1) Shutterstock Images/KIM NGUYEN; p. 43: (2) Shutterstock Images/jantarus; p. 43: (3) Shutterstock Images/Olga Popova; p. 43: (5) Shutterstock Images/Naufal MQ; p. 43: (6) Shutterstock Images/annadarzy; p. 43: (7) Shutterstock Images/KIM NGUYEN; p. 43: (8) Shutterstock Images/Michal Nowosielski; p. 43: (9) Shutterstock Images/Hurst Photo; p. 43: (10) Shutterstock Images/Nagritsamon Ruksujjar; p. 43: (12) Shutterstock Images/VladaKela; p. 43: (13) Shutterstock Images/indigolotos; p. 43: (14) Shutterstock Images/Gregory Gerber; p. 43: (11) Shutterstock Images/Dancestrokes: p. 43: (3) Alamy/©Michael Flippo: p. 43: (4) Shutterstock Images/Blue Pig; p. 43: (15) Shutterstock Images/nioloxs; p. 44: (L) ©Manzo Niikura/amanaimages/Corbis; p. 44: (TC) Shutterstock Images/BestPhotoStudio: p. 44: (1) Alamy/©Photocuisine; p. 44: (C) Shutterstock Images/Sabphoto; p. 44: (3) Alamy/©Michael Flippo; p. 44: (CR) Cambridge University Press/RBP; p. 46: (BR) Superstock/imageBROKER; p. 46: (TL) Shutterstock Images/nioloxs; p. 46: (BL) Alamy/©Realimage; p. 47: (CL) Shutterstock Images/Nitr; p. 48: (1) Getty Images/Tony C French Calc; p. 48: (2) Alamy/©Rob Cousins; p. 48: (3) Alamy/©Lazyllama; p. 48: (4) Alamy/©Jim West; p. 49: (B/G) Alamy/©Rob Cousins: p. 49: (T) Shutterstock Images/Rob Marmion: p. 49: (TC) Shutterstock Images/Piyato: p. 49: (C) Shutterstock Images/HLPhoto; p. 50: (BR) Gareth Boden; p. 50: (TR) Shutterstock Images/XiXinXing; p. 51: (L) Alamy/©Robert Marmion; p. 54: (B/G) Shutterstock Images/Sylvie Bouchard; p. 56: (TL) Fotosearch / SuperStock; p. 56: (C) Alamy/©tbkmedia.de; p. 56: (TR) ©Joe McDonald/Corbis; p. 56: (CR) Thomas Marent/Minden Pictures/FLPA; p. 56: (BR) Jevgenija Pigozne/ImageBROKER/Glowimages; p. 56: (5) Glow Images/Jevgenija Pigozne/ImageBROKER; p. 57: (CL) Frans Lanting/FLPA; p. 58: (TR) Alamy/©frans lemmens; p. 58: (6) Shutterstock Images/Jeff Dalton; p. 58: (5) Shutterstock Images/Shane Myers Photography; p. 58: (1) Alamy/©Juniors Bildarchiv GmbH; p. 58: (7) SuperStock/Biosphoto; p. 58: (3) SuperStock/NHPA; p. 58: (4) Minden Pictures/Masterfile; p. 58: (2) SuperStock/Frank Sommariva/image/imagebroker.net; p. 58: (TR) SuperStock/©National Geographic; p. 58: (1) Alamy/©Juniors Bildarchiv GmbH; p. 58: (2) SuperStock /©Frank Sommariva/imagebroker.net; p. 58: (3) SuperStock/©NHPA; p. 58: (4) Alamy/©blickwinkel; p. 58: (5) Shutterstock Images/idreamphoto; p. 58: (6) Shutterstock Images/Mark Lehigh; p. 58: (7) SuperStock/©Biosphoto; p. 59: (BL) Alamy/©Gabriel Rif; p. 60: (1) Alamy/©Arco Images GmbH; p. 60: (2) Shutterstock Images/ArCaLu; p. 60: (3) Shutterstock Images/TTshutter; p. 60: (4) Shutterstock Images/Sergey Uryadnikov; p. 60: (5) Shutterstock Images/Petra Christen; p. 60: (6) Shutterstock Images/eAlisa; p. 61: (T) Getty Images/Wayne R Bilenduke; p. 61: (BR) SuperStock/imagebroker.net; p. 62: (1) Alamy/©LOOK Die Bildagentur der Fotografen GmbH; p. 62: (2) Alamy/©Greg Balfour Evans; p. 62: (3) Alamy/©Jeff Morgan 09; p. 63: (TR) Alamy/©Arletta Cwalina; p. 64: (B/G) Getty Images/Martin Puddy; p. 65: (3) Alamy/©Andrew Fox; p. 65: (4) ©Randy Faris/Corbis; p. 65: (5) SuperStock/©Flirt; p. 65: (6) SuperStock/Tony Garcia; p. 65: (7) Alamy/©Bubbles Photolibrary; p. 65: (1) Alamy/©Stock Connection Blue; p. 65: (2) Alamy/©Radius Images; p. 65: (5) SuperStock/©Flirt; p. 66: (B/G) Alamy/©Ammit; p. 66: (TR) Tony Waltham/Robert

Harding; p. 66: (CT) Alamy/©Robert Harding Picture Library Ltd; p. 66: (CB) SuperStock/Peter Barritt/Robert Harding Picture Library; p. 70: (2) Alamy/©Ron Yue; p. 70: (4) Shutterstock Images/T Anderson; p. 70: (5) Shutterstock Images/Radiokafka; p. 70: (4) Shutterstock Images/T Anderson; p. 70: (2) Alamy©Ron Yue; p. 70: (3) Shutterstock Images/BaLL LunLa; p. 70: (5) Shutterstock Images/Radiokafka; p. 70: (B/G) Shutterstock Images/ER_09; p. 70: (6) Shutterstock Images/Baloncici; p. 71: (1) age fotostock/©keng po leung/Kalium Collection; p. 71: (2) Alamy/©discpicture; p. 71: (3) Alamy/©Doug Houghton Asia; p. 71: (4) Alamy/©Jon Bower Hong Kong; p. 71: (5) Shutterstock Images/Songquan Deng; p. 72: (1) Alamy/©Golden Pixels LLC; p. 72: (2) Alamy/©Jeff Greenberg 5 of 6; p. 72: (a) SuperStock/©Comstock/Exactostock; p. 72: (b) Shutterstock Images/Darren; p. 72: (d) Masterfile/R. Ian Lloyd; p. 72: (c) Alamy/©Lenscap; p. 73: (T) Alamy/©Bryan Eveleigh; p. 73: (inset) Alamy/©imageBROKER; p. 76: (B/G) Alamy/©Aurora Photos; p. 77: (1) Shutterstock Images/StacieStauffSmith Photos; p. 77: (2) Alamy/©Joe Belanger; p. 77: (6) Alamy/©Shaun Wilkinson; p. 77: (10) Alamy/©Andres Rodriguez; p. 77: (3) Shutterstock Images/Tom Gowanlock; p. 77: (4) Shutterstock Images/Radu Razvan; p. 77: (5) Shutterstock Images/gorillaimages; p. 77: (8) Alamy/©Aflo Foto Agency; p. 77: (9) Nick Vangopoulos/Thinkstock; p. 77: (7) Shutterstock Images/EcoPrint; p. 77: (2) Shutterstock Images/Andrey_Popov; p. 77: (1) Shutterstock Images/StacieStauffSmith Photos; p. 77: (11) Getty Images/Happy to share the beauty I see in my travels; p. 77: (7) Shutterstock Images/EcoPrint; p. 77: (10) Alamy/©Andres Rodriguez; p. 78: (T) Shutterstock Images/J. Henning Buchholz; p. 80: (a) Shutterstock Images/Neveshkin Nikolay; p. 80: (b) Shutterstock Images/Elnur; p. 80: (b) Shutterstock Images/Elnur; p. 80: (c) Shutterstock Images/Karkas; p. 80: (d) Shutterstock Images/Alexander Kalina; p. 80: (e) Shutterstock Images/Elnur; p. 80: (f) Shutterstock Images/mimon!; p. 80: (g) Shutterstock Images/Petar Djordjevic; p. 80: (h) Shutterstock Images/In Green; p. 80: (i) Shutterstock Images/Vlue; p. 80: (i) Shutterstock Images/Karkas; p. 80: (k) Shutterstock Images/Vlue; p. 80: (l) Alamy/©D. Hurst; p. 80: (d) Shutterstock Images/Alexander Kalina; p. 80: (e) Shutterstock Images/Elnur; p. 80: (g) Alamy/©JASON BATTERHAM; p. 80: (h) Shutterstock Images/In Green; p. 80: (j) Shutterstock Images/prostok; p. 80: (k) Shutterstock Images/Vlue;p. 81: (c) Shutterstock Images/Karkas; p. 81: (f) Shutterstock Images/mimon!; p. 81: (i) Shutterstock Images/Elnur; p. 81: (L) Alamy/©D. Hurst; p. 82: (T) age fotostock/©John Woodworth/Loop Images; p. 83: (a) © DAVID GRAY/Reuters/Corbis; p. 83: (b) ©Mark Bryan Makela/In Pictures/Corbis; p. 83: (c) Getty Images/Jim Richardson; p. 83: (d) Alamy/©Mar Photographics; p. 84: (1) SuperStock/©Image Source; p. 85: (T) Alamy/©epa european pressphoto agency b.v.; p. 85: (T) Alamy/©epa european pressphoto agency b.v.; p. 86-87: (B/G) Getty Images/Matthew Micah Wright; p. 87: (TL) Alamy/©Gay Bumgarner; p. 87: (1) Alamy/©Angie Sharp; p. 87: (2) PETER SKINNER/SCIENCE PHOTO LIBRARY; p. 87: (3) Alamy/©Juniors Bildarchiv GmbH; p. 87: (4) London News Pictures/Rex Features; p. 87: (5) Alamy/©Fredrick Kippe; p. 87: (6) Alamy/©Design Pics Inc.; p. 87: (7) ©Radius Images/Corbis; p. 87: (8) Shutterstock Images/bruno ismael da silva alves; p. 88: (B/G) Alamy/©Celia Mannings; p. 88: (TR) Shutterstock Images/clearviewstock; p. 88: (CR) Jacek Chabraszewski/Thinkstock; p. 88: (TL) Alamy/©Blend Images; p. 88: (BL) Alamy/©MBI; p. 88: (2) Shutterstock Images/Dmytro Vietrov; p. 88: (6) SuperStock/©NHPA; p. 89: (T) Alamy/©Gary Dublanko; p. 90: (1) SuperStock/©Steve Vidler; p. 90: (2) SuperStock/©Visions of America; p. 90: (B/G) ©Gavin Hellier/JAI/Corbis; p. 90: (3) Shutterstock Images/dibrova; p. 91: (bottom) Shutterstock Images/finallast; p. 92: (a) Shutterstock Images/Vitalii Nesterchuk; p. 92: (b) Alamy/©david sanger photography; p. 92: (c) Alamy/©Tetra Images; p. 92: (d) SuperStock/©Tips Images; p. 93: (1) SuperStock/©Juice Images; p. 93: (2) Alamy/© ZUMA Press: Inc.; p. 93: (3) Newscom/Design Pics/Kevin Smith; p. 93: (4) Shutterstock Images/Ferenc Szelepcsenyi; p. 93: (5) Alamy/©Universal Images Group Limited; p. 94: (CL) Alamy/©Robert Fried; p. 90: (CR) Shutterstock Images/Monkey Business Images; p. 94: (BC) Shutterstock Images/YanLev; p. 94: (1) Alamy/©Barry Lewis; p. 95: (T) Gavin Hellier/Robert Harding; p. 107: (TR) Shutterstock Images/Olesia Bilkei; p. 108: (TR) Shutterstock Images/Gst; p. 110: (TR) Shutterstock Images/Nexus 7; p. 111: (TR) Shutterstock Images/Potapov Alexander; p. 112: (TC) Alamy/©Andrew Fox; p. 112: (C) ©Randy Faris/Corbis; p. 112: (CL) SuperStock/©Flirt; p. 112: (BL) SuperStock/Tony Garcia; p. 112: (CR) Alamy/©Bubbles Photolibrary; p. 112: (TR) Alamy/©Stock Connection Blue; p. 112: (BR) Alamy/©Radius Images; p. 113: (TR) Shutterstock Images/Bojanovic; p. 113: (BR) Shutterstock Images/Ksusha Dusmikeeva; p. 114: (TR) Shutterstock Images/sRenee; p. 118: (3) Shutterstock Images/Artem Samokhvalov: p. 118: (6) Shutterstock Images/VladislavGudovskiy: p. 118: (4) Shutterstock Images/Diana Taliun: p. 118: (1) Shutterstock Images/Olyina: p. 118: (5) Shutterstock Images/KIM NGUYEN: p. 118: (2) Shutterstock Images/EM Arts; p. 123: (T) fStop / SuperStock; p. 124: (L) Alamy/©AgStock Images, Inc.; p. 124: (C) IMAGEBROKER,ALFRED & ANNALIESE T/Imagebroker/FLPA; p. 124: (R) Tim Fitzharris/Minden Pictures/FLPA; p. 125: (B/G) Getty Images/Laurie Noble; p. 125: (R) Shutterstock Images/frescomovie; p. 125: (C) Alamy/©Robert Harding World Imagery.

The publishers are grateful to the following illustrators:
Janet Allinger p. 46; Giorgio Bacchin (Beehive Illustration) p. 80; David Belmonte (Beehive Illustration) p. 61, 66, 125; Nigel Dobbyn (Beehive Illustration) p. 68, 81; Mark Duffin p. 4, 33, 109; Bob Lea p. 14, 55; Andrew Painter p. 6 (R), 13; Q2A Media Services Inc. p. 6 (BL), 8, 16, 26, 27, 36, 38, 47, 48, 49, 62, 71, 83, 92, 93, 101; Martin Sanders (Beehive Illustration) p. 22; David Shephard (Bright Agency) p. 5, 34, 45; Sean Tiffany p. 6 (BR), 15, 79.

All video stills by kind permission of:
Discovery Communications, LLC 2015:10 (1, 2, 4), 13, 16, 20 (1, 2, 4), 23, 26, 32 (1, 2, 4), 35, 38, 42 (1, 2, 4), 45, 48, 54 (1, 2, 4), 57, 60, 64 (1, 2, 4), 67, 70, 76 (1, 2, 4), 79, 82, 86 (1, 2, 4), 89, 92, 115, 116, 117, 118, 119, 120, 121, 122.
Cambridge University Press: 9, 10 (3), 18, 20 (3), 28, 32 (3), 40, 42 (3), 50, 54 (3), 62, 64 (3), 72, 76 (3), 84, 86 (3), 94.

Development of this publication has made use of the Cambridge English Corpus (CEC). The CEC is a computer database of contemporary spoken and written English, which currently stands at over one billion words. It includes British English, American English and other varieties of English. It also includes the Cambridge Learner Corpus, developed in collaboration with the University of Cambridge ESOL Examinations. Cambridge University Press has built up the CEC to provide evidence about language use that helps to produce better language teaching materials.

The publishers are grateful to the following contributors:
Blooberry: concept design
emc design limited: text design and layouts
QBS: cover design and photo selection
Ian Harker and Dave Morritt: audio recordings
Integra: video production
Nick Bruckman and People's TV: voxpop video production
Citivox and Hart McCleod: video voiceovers
Anna Whitcher: video management
BraveArts, S.L: additional audio recordings
Getty Images: music
Vicki Anderson: Speaking and Writing pages
Sam Lewis: CLIL pages
Alice Martin: Starter Unit and Project pages